How to
FIND, EVALUATE, AND BUY A LAUNDROMAT

Jason Lombardo

SPECIAL THANKS

First and foremost I would like to thank Joe. You planted the seed and had all the tools to make this happen. Even if I would have come up with this idea on my own, I wouldn't know how to execute it. To my mother and stepfather who have encouraged entrepreneurship and supported me with all my business ventures good and bad throughout the years. Also to my wife Stephanie for always believing in me and giving me that little extra push when needed. I wouldn't be able to accomplish anything without you.

CONTENTS

SPECIAL NOTE

This edition of "How to Find, Evaluate and Buy a Laundromat" is strictly for educational purposes. The author and publisher have used their best efforts in preparing this publication, but make no representation or warranty with respect to the accuracy, applicability, fitness, or completeness of the contents. There is no guarantee that you will earn any money using the techniques and ideas in this publication. Therefore, if you wish to apply the ideas contained in this publication, you are taking full responsibility for your actions.

No warranties or guarantees are expressed or implied by the publisher's choice to include any of the content in this volume.

Neither the publisher nor the author shall be liable for any physical, psychological, emotional, financial, or commercial damages, including, but not limited to special, incidental, consequential or other damages. Before buying any business, you should consult with an attorney, an accountant and a business professional.

PREFACE

I should start by admitting that this book wasn't my idea.

You see, I belong to a networking group that meets occasionally for lunch, and once in a while, we actually talk business. When this is the case, I often talk about how I regularly encounter different laundromats that are up for sale and the research I do to find out if the business is worth pursuing.

I told them how I would use the Internet to look up all of the property tax records and water bills for the laundromat in question. Then, I would visit the laundromat, take count of the equipment and vend prices, and use a water usage spreadsheet to figure out how much business the store was doing by backing in off of the water bill.

My networking buddies found these practices interesting and had a lot of questions. They wanted to know how I knew how much water a washer uses, how I found out their water usage and bills without them knowing, and how I knew if the laundry owner was past due on his water bill.

After I explained it all, some of them suggested that I write a book on everything people needed to know if they wanted to buy a laundromat. This conversation went on for about a year before finally, one night after a few beers, I agreed to write the how-to guide you have in front of you.

Another reason I decided to take on this project was because a new laundromat had recently opened its doors down the road from my business. When I first found this out, I went on a bit of a rampage to find what my next steps should be in order to stay competitive. I really started to drive myself a little nuts and I was losing sleep. I just couldn't find any good information out there on what exactly to do. As a result, I was forced to come up with my own plan, which I share with you in this book.

Unfortunately, for me it took the shock of a new competitor to really motivate me into improving my laundry. Of course, I had been making gradual improvements to my business before this, but the thought of losing out to another business made me really kick it into high gear.

I should also mention that I am not a writer. I'm a laundromat owner/operator and a landlord, and I always try to do everything for myself. For now I am self employed and loving it, and I really enjoy being hands-on. Someday I would like to be a business owner who stands back and lets other people handle the details. It may never happen, but I try to develop my plans around that idea.

This book is a good read if you are looking for an existing laundromat to purchase or would just like to improve one that you already have. It will cover the many aspects of finding, evaluating, buying, and owning a laundromat.

I should also note that one topic we won't cover is building a new laundromat. This is because it's very difficult to start from scratch and generate cash flow right away. If you are paying cash or have a very large down payment, you are going to increase your odds. However, in most cases you could spend anywhere from $500,000 to $1 million or more to build and you could end up losing money from months to years. You have to earn every customer one by one and keep them. And who's to say that the other laundromats in the area aren't going to remodel once they learn of the new competition?

For this reason, I advise against building a new laundromat and instead urge you to consider purchasing one that's already in operation.

If you purchase an existing laundromat – even if it's a dump – you'll have customers on day one. Your next goal should be to improve the business by making it feel safe, secure, and clean and addressing any issues associated with the laundromat. By advertising and letting people know about the new owner and new look of the business, your bottom line will continue to improve.

I have also included a chapter on what to do if new competition moves in. As I mentioned earlier, that's when I really kicked it into high gear. I packed a lot of information into this chapter and it's a must read for everyone. We must be prepared for all of the potential "what ifs" that may arise.

I have developed numerous spreadsheets over the years to assist me with my business quests, some examples of which I have included in this book. These include a pro-forma, a profit and loss statement, collection sheets, a turn forecast sheet with water usage, and more. They are also available for purchase on my website at HowToBuyaLaundromat.com if you see any you'd like to try.

Remember, there are many different ways to find, evaluate, and improve a laundromat. The method in this book is simply the way that I have done it, with much success. Some people may disagree with my approach. I encourage you to research all of the methods out there and find the one that best fits your needs.

Finally, keep in mind that an investment in a laundromat is not guaranteed and there is risk involved. It's risk verses reward, but I suggest calculating that risk up front to increase your odds of success.

So, with that in mind, are you ready to embark on a laundromat adventure? If so, let's get started.

CHAPTER 1
MY START IN THE BIZ

In order to truly understand the information in this book, I should tell you a little about myself and how I got started in the laundry business.

It all started when I got fired after 10 years in the car business as a finance manager. At the time I wasn't happy with my job and had started looking for other options. Eventually my boss found out and I was let go the day after I went on a job interview.

I immediately filed for unemployment and tried to figure out what to do next. My wife had gone back to college and was only working part time, and I had my kids, a nice middle-class home, and all the bills everyone else has. I needed to prioritize, keep my wife in school, cancel everything I didn't need, and get a job.

By that time, the car business was losing steam and I knew that I didn't want to go back to doing the same thing. So, I tried to use my finance experience to get a job at a bank as a credit buyer or auto finance lender. Although I had some good contacts in the banking industry, my countless resumes and phone calls were all in vein. In this desperate situation, I started looking into buying a business.

I had been trying to start a successful business for a while. I had been a partner in an auto salvage business for a short time, had started an eBay business, and had purchased some rental properties. These ventures had varied levels of success, as I still own the rental properties, my ex-partner still runs the salvage business with much success, and the eBay experiment never made any money.

My initial thought was that I was going to be a full-time landlord, but I soon realized that it takes time to earn money in the real estate business. The only way to really make a profit was to own a lot of properties and I wasn't in the position to buy fifty units right off the bat.

To maximize my efforts, I purchased all the usual start-up magazines and searched the Internet up and down. I ended up finding a radiator franchise that looked promising, but after months of research and finally mustering the courage to pull the trigger, someone else beat me to the punch and bought the place I was considering. At that point I was back to square one and time was running out. I was beginning to think I would have to cash out my 401(k) to live on instead of using it to start a business.

Just when I thought my options had run out, I found a small laundromat for sale just around the corner from my house. I had always thought about owning a laundry, so it was a good opportunity. After all, I had heard stories about this guy or that guy who owned a laundromat and had lots of money and not a care in the world. I figured it was a chance worth taking.

My previous experience in business taught me how to look at profit and loss (P & L) statements and to project earnings using a pro-forma. After crunching the numbers, I figured I would have about $400 to bank after all of the expenses, assuming that I cash in my 401(k) and have no debt service. In keeping with my "glass half full" personality, I was confident that I could do better than the current owner and was about to make my move to buy the laundromat.

Throughout this due diligence I made some contacts in the industry, including distributors. Now, I had been in sales a long time, so I quickly learned how this was going to work.

"This is a good location but it needs new dryers or more efficient washers," they would say. I don't mean to bad mouth distributors because I have learned a lot from them, but you do need to think for yourself and use realistic numbers when trying to project new revenue.

That being said, the location I was looking at did need new equipment, but I just didn't know it at the time. On top of that, this place made very little money to begin with, so if I were to buy it and put in new equipment, I would have to produce a lot more revenue to break even with my new loan.

It soon became apparent that I would need to own about 10 small laundromats to make any kind of living, which I couldn't afford.

A little while later, I was speaking with my parents about my grim job prospects, my failed franchise ideas, and the small laundry around the corner. My step-father mentioned a friend of his from high school who owned a laundromat and was looking to sell, although this had been several months earlier. As it turned out, his friend had not yet sold his business, but was about to receive an offer. After a brief phone conversation, he agreed to let me visit the laundromat on Thanksgiving morning while the business was closed and he was doing some maintenance.

We talked about his business and how he got started. About 13 years earlier, he had built the laundromat after being laid off. Not long after, he was scooped up by another firm, so he and his wife used it for supplemental income. His wife did most of the management of the business, but she wanted it sold so she could spend more time with her grandchildren.

I should note that this was no ordinary laundromat. It had attendants staffed from open to close and services that included coin laundry, tanning, dry cleaning, drop laundry, and a seamstress. It was a good-sized place, taking up about 4,500 square feet, and I was already thinking of ways I could improve it.

The place looked dated, with carpet throughout and up the walls leading to a chair rail. There were handwritten signs everywhere and everything just looked old. The couple had been running a good business, but they had been doing it on the cheap.

Knowing that he was looking to get out of the business, I asked if he would accept an offer from me if the other bid he was expecting fell through. He agreed, and as it turned out, he never received the other offer. This came as no surprise, he told me, as several people had been interested but were unable to get the money together.

Money was also a problem for me. I had no idea how I was going to pay for the business and knew that I would have to get a loan. This would be tricky, considering I had no job, no industry experience, and no luck at the time. What I did have was determination and a lot of time on my hands.

After a little back and forth, he accepted my offer. We had to jump through a few hoops and deal with some unexpected challenges, like a difficult landlord and utility security deposits, but we closed on the sale. I was officially a laundromat owner.

CHAPTER 2
LAUNDRY LINGO

Before we embark on finding a laundromat that's for sale, we first should go over some business and laundry industry terms. Understanding this lingo will make it easier to understand this book and the laundry business in general. For example, if you are talking to a seller of a laundromat and she says that she improved her turns from three to four on her triples and that increased her annual gross by $10,000, you need to know what she is talking about.

Getting to know these terms will make it easier to navigate through this book:

CARD SYSTEM: A method of payment that uses a prepaid card, much like a credit or debit card. This type of system will have a main terminal in which a customer inserts their money or credit card to receive a laundry card that can be swiped at each washer and dryer. These systems are great from a management standpoint and can be programmed easily to do specials and promotions. There may be some customer training involved.

CENTUM CUBIC FEET (CCF): Typical unit in which industrial-consumption of natural gas or water is measured. Each CCF equals 100 cubic-feet.

DEBT SERVICE: The series of payments of interest and principal required on a debt over a given period of time.

DISTRIBUTOR: A person who sells commercial laundry equipment. They generally have a territory in which they can sell.

DOUBLE LOAD WASHER: A front load washer in which two loads can be washed at once. This could be an 18 lb. or 20 lb. washer.

DROP OFF: Also known as "wash and fold" or "fluff and fold." Laundromats will charge by the pound to spot treat, wash, dry, fold, and package a customer's laundry.

Dryer Pocket: The term for one dryer. A stack dryer has two dryer pockets, one on top of the other. For example, 10 stack dryers would have a total of 20 dryer pockets.

DUE DILIGENCE: A term used for a number of concepts involving the investigation of a business. It can be a legal obligation, but the term more commonly applies to voluntary investigations. A common example of due diligence is the process through which a potential acquirer evaluates a target company or its assets before acquisition.

FRONT LOAD WASHER: A washing machine that is loaded from the front. They come in many sizes, including 18 lb., 20 lb., 30 lb., 35 lb., 40 lb., 50 lb., 60 lb., and 80 lb. capacity washers.

GROSS LEASE: A property lease in which the landlord agrees to pay all expenses normally associated with ownership, such as utilities, repairs, insurance, and (sometimes) taxes. In a gross lease your rent will not change for an agreed-upon period of time, even if the owner's expenses increase.

GROSS SALES: The total of all sales before deductions or expenses.

IMPACT FEES: The fee a municipality will charge for each washer being hooked up to the sewer line. These are also called sewer connection fees and washer hook-up fees.

LAUNDROMAT: I probably don't need to define this word, but from time to time I will call a laundromat a "laundry." Sometimes I even call it a "store." This drives my wife crazy, which is why I keep doing it.

MAKE-UP AIR: Air brought into a building from outside through ventilation to replace exhaust air. Dryers need adequate make-up air to operate efficiently.

NET PROFIT: Often referred to as the bottom line, net profit is calculated by subtracting a company's total expenses from total revenue or gross sales, thus showing what the company has earned (or lost) in a given period of time. We strive for a lot of net profit.

PROFIT AND LOSS STATEMENT: An account compiled at the end of an accounting period to show gross and net profit (or loss).

PRO-FORMA: An analysis of expected income and expenses for a business that is for sale.

PULL: The process of collecting coins from a machine.

ROUTE OPERATOR: A person or organization who services and/or manages laundry equipment in residential buildings, such as in apartments or condos.

STACKED DRYER: A dryer that has two dryers on top of one another in a cabinet.

TOP LOAD WASHER: A washer that loads from the top. I sometimes refer to them as "tops."

TRIPLE LOAD WASHER: A front load washer in which three loads can be washed at once. This could be a 30 lb. or a 35 lb. washer.

TRIPLE-NET LEASE: A lease in which the lessee pays rent to the landlord, as well as all taxes, insurance, and mainte-nance expenses that arise from use of the property. If the landlord's taxes, insurance, or maintenance go up, so does that part of the rent. This amount can increase or decrease from year to year.

TUMBLER: The drum inside of a washer or dryer.

TURN: One use of a washer or dryer.

TURNS PER DAY (TPD): The number of times a washer or dryer is used in a single day.

Throughout this book, I use these terms frequently. Be sure to check back to this chapter for definitions.

CHAPTER 3
HOW TO FIND A LAUNDROMAT FOR SALE

So you've decided to take the plunge and start the process of becoming a laundromat owner. While there are many great things about this business, it may not be as easy as you think. This book will help you along the way, but first things first – we need to learn how to find a laundry that's for sale.

CHECK THE LOCAL LISTINGS

I started this process by looking in the local paper. The newspaper is a great source for information and I still check it every day. Another great source is the Internet, which has a ton of information on just about anything business-related. One of my favorite sites is BizBuySell.com, which features up-to-date information on all kinds of businesses, including laundromats. If you sign up with the site they send you new listings for free.

Every once in a while I also get lucky with CraigsList.com, where owners can post a business that's for sale. Most posters use it to test the market to see if they get any interest. This is helpful because it's possible to get a better deal by working with the business owners directly rather than going through a business broker or real estate agent and the commission that comes with it.

However, at times a broker might be the best option. Business brokers, real estate agents, or (in some cases) laundry brokers work for the seller, but have a lot of resources at their disposal. They can be found by looking in the yellow pages or on the Internet. With real estate agents, you can check to see if there are any businesses for sale by checking your local multiple listing service (MLS) website.

In most cases, when you deal with a real estate agent or broker, you'll have to sign a confidentiality agreement. They don't want to take the chance of you talking to an employee or someone you shouldn't be talking to.

NETWORK WITH THE PROS

Have you ever heard that most businesses that are for sale never go on the market? It's true. So how do we tap into those if we never even know their available?

We need to be creative.

In order to know about the most prized businesses up for sale, you must network with some industry professionals and talk to some owners and service people. The service people in particular seem to know everything about everybody, so you should get to know them. As for owners, attending an industry trade show will connect you with them. They might not be selling, but they'll know someone who is.

To get into a trade show, find out who the laundry distributors are in your area.

Every brand of commercial laundry equipment has a distributor. They sell and service equipment, build laundromats, manage laundromats, build and manage laundry rooms in apartment buildings, rehab and sell laundromats, and sell parts and supplies. Not all distributors do all of these things, but there are some that do it all. Most distributors are trustworthy people, but there are those who are not, so be aware. Be careful and use your own judgment.

The best way to find who the distributors are is to check the yellow pages or join the Coin Laundry Association (CLA). The CLA's website is CoinLaundry.org. This organization has a ton of information for everyone in the industry and those looking to break into it. They also have a trade magazine that features a classified section in which you can find a listing of laundromats for sale. It's a nationwide listing, but you might get lucky and find one that's local.

Distributors are usually more than happy to have you at a trade show, so don't be afraid to ask. The distributors themselves may have some laundries in inventory that they have rehabbed. Many times, they can line you up with potential sellers.

Be sure to give the owners you meet your number and let them know that you're in the market to buy and ask them to call you if they hear of anything becoming available. It helps to have a card with your information prepared in advance. Naturally, the more professional you are the better.

The reason giving out your number is important is that, as a laundry owner, I know that I wouldn't tell someone at a trade show if I knew something was available. In fact, right now I know of at least six businesses that are for sale in my city. However, I would call later and give information on those that I decided to pass on. Just because I passed doesn't mean it's not a good laundry. I may have passed on it because it's simply too far from my house.

Remember, the reason that I know of the laundries that are available is because I've networked and everyone knows that I regularly am looking to buy. Networking generates some good leads for me.

GO FOR A DRIVE

This probably seems obvious, but another good way to find laundromats on the market is to drive around and look. Although many businesses for sale are never advertised as such, still more sit on the market for a long time without any buyers. This is true even for very desirable locations, especially in a down economy.

Be sure to tell your friends to keep an eye out, especially if they drive around a lot. One of my good friends is a police officer who is on the road every day, so I ask him to watch for businesses that are for sale. If he sees any or hears of any problems, he is sure to let me know. I have recently been able to find four laundries I heard about through friends.

You can learn a lot of valuable information via word of mouth. For example, I currently know of two laundromats that have had fires and are now closed. What if their insurance doesn't cover the loss? It could be an opportunity.

I also know of two more laundromats that were vandalized and recently closed. One of them has new equipment on the way, but the owner is tired of it and wants to sell. These are the types of opportunities you cannot afford to miss.

LETTERS OF INTEREST

One more way that I found to create some good leads is to write a letter of interest and send it to the owners of every laundromat in the city. This letter needs to be short and to the point. Here is an example:

Dear Laundry Owner,

My name is John Doe. I am writing you because I am looking for a laundromat to purchase in Sample City or the surrounding area. I am not a broker. I am just an investor who is in search of a business. I will look at any size, attended or unattended laundromat. This includes real estate or leased space. It does not matter if the laundromat is in excellent condition or needs work.

You can reach me at 000-000-0000. If I do not answer, please leave a message and I will call you right back.

Thank you for your time,

John Doe

You'll get your phone ringing with a letter like this. Most of the calls will be from owners whose laundries are in some pretty bad situations, but sometimes you'll find a good one. It is definitely worth a try.

In most cases, you can send the letter directly to the laundromat. Look in your phone book and online to get addresses to most of the laundries in your area. However, you might find that some laundromats that you know of are not listed anywhere. Find the address by driving by and writing it down.

Some of the letters you send will get returned due to there being no postal box at the address, so you will have to go inside to see if they have a license on the wall. The license will have a name and address on it. It may be a business name or a person's name, but it will usually be a good mailing address.

Above all, you need to be patient. It may take a while for you to find the right laundromat. I wouldn't rush the process, but instead take your time and do your due diligence. Some people are able to find the right laundromat relatively quickly, while for others it takes longer, perhaps a few years.

CHAPTER 4
TOTALING A LAUNDROMAT'S SALES

Now that we know the lingo and how to find a laundromat that is for sale, we can start looking. However, before we begin talking with laundry owners, we need to know a couple things.

Namely, we need the answers to questions like: How do they count their money? How do they track turns per day (TPD)? Does the seller even track TPD?

Knowing this information will be invaluable as you conduct your search of laundromats potentially worth buying. This chapter not only shows you how to find the answers, but will also provide helpful tips for when you begin running your own laundromat.

HOW DO THEY COUNT THEIR MONEY?

If the seller has a card store, the process will be different than if it is a coin store. In most cases, a card store will have financial software that comes with the system, providing an audit trail or documentation of the laundromat's sales. This makes things easy for owners, as it allows them to print off profit and loss statements and TPD information at the click of a mouse.

With a card system you still have to fill the terminal with cards, get software updates, and collect paper cash from the terminal, but you won't have to deal with quarters. This helps simplify things and makes a lot of sense from a management standpoint. However, information from a card system still needs to be verified.

If the seller has a coin store, the process is a little different and perhaps a bit more difficult to understand at first. With coins, owners have to collect the quarters from each machine and tally the sales manually.

Counting coins can be done using a couple of different methods. The most common is to weigh the coins with a coin scale. I have found this to be the best option for most. Another method is to use a coin counter, into which coins are inserted like the machines at the bank. In my opinion, this usually takes too long and is less efficient than simply weighing the coins.

You can find currency scales on the market that are extremely accurate, but I just use my wash and fold scale and multiply the weight (in pounds) by $19.90, which is what a pound of quarters weighs. We use that number because $19.75 weighs slightly less than one pound, so we have to add a partial quarter to reach it exactly. When there are several pounds involved, the partial quarters add up, and in the end I simply round up or down to the nearest quarter. The process isn't perfect, but it's close enough.

There are different benefits and downfalls to both the card and coin options, so I will let you come to your own conclusion as to which you prefer. Personally, I feel that coin and card have both worked well for me.

HOW DO THEY TRACK TURNS PER DAY (TPD)?

Tracking TPD requires a table on a sheet of paper on which you can list each type of washer and dryer, like the one provided below. Sometimes I collect on different days of the week, so it's important to have columns for each day, with five weeks on a collection sheet so that it works for any month. It's useful because I can look back at previous years to see when and how much I collected. This form is also available on my website.

MONTH/YEAR

Week One	Sunday	Monday	Tuesday	Wednesday	Thursday	Friday	Saturday	Totals
Tops								
Doubles								
Triples								
50lb Washers								
60lb Washers								
30lb Dryers								
50lb Dryers								
Vending								
Total								

To keep things straight, I always collect all of the coins from one type of washer or dryer first, then move on to the others. This makes recordkeeping easier for me.

For example, let's say we're collecting the quarters from each top load washer and that we're weighing the coins. If we have 15.6 pounds of quarters from our ten top load washers, we can calculate our sales for the week:

15.6 lbs. x \$19.90 = \$310.44 (round up to \$310.50)

This is our pull from the top load washers for the week. To find turns per day, we need to know some additional information, such as the vending price for each of our ten top load washers. Let's say it's \$1.50 per wash. To calculate, first take the total sales divided by the number of washers:

\$310.50 / 10 = \$31.05 (This is the average amount each machine took in for the week.)

Then, divide that number by the vending price:

31.05 / 1.50 = 20.7 (This is the average number of turns per week for each machine.)

To find the TPD, divide that number by seven for the number of days in the week:

20.7 / 7 = 2.95

We have now figured that our average TPD is 2.95, which means that our top load washers are used for approximately three cycles each day. We can repeat this process for each of the washers and dryers.

Usually while I'm at the laundromat, I only record the pounds of coins collected and figure the rest out in the comfort of my office. When searching for a laundromat to buy, ask the owner how he or she records this information.

Below is my "Month in Review," into which I enter my pounds:

Year	2011	Month	April				
Days for Count		7	7	7	7	3	31
lbs	# of Units	Week 1	Week 2	Week 3	Week 4	Week 5	Month
60lb Washer	2	15.2	14.8	14	15.8	7.4	67.2
30lb Washer	6	36.6	33.6	30.8	34.6	15.8	151.4
30lb Dryer	20	49.2	47.8	44.2	48	24.6	213.8
50lb Dryer	4	6.4	5.2	5.2	6.2	3	26
Double	5	8.8	7.2	6.8	8.8	3.6	35.2
Top Loader	15	22.2	21	20.6	20.6	9.6	94
Total		138.4	129.6	121.6	134	64	587.6

Sales		Week 1	Week 2	Week 3	Week 4	Week 5	Month
60lb Washer		$302.48	$294.52	$278.60	$314.42	$147.26	$1,337.28
30lb Washer		$728.34	$668.64	$612.92	$688.54	$314.42	$3,012.86
30lb Dryer		$979.08	$951.22	$879.58	$955.20	$489.54	$4,254.62
50lb Dryer		$127.36	$103.48	$103.48	$123.38	$59.70	$517.40
Double		$175.12	$143.28	$135.32	$175.12	$71.64	$700.48
Top Loader		$441.78	$417.90	$409.94	$409.94	$191.04	$1,870.60
Total		$2,754.16	$2,579.04	$2,419.84	$2,666.60	$1,273.60	$11,693.24

Turns	Vend Price	Week 1	Week 2	Week 3	Week 4	Week 5	Month
60lb Washer	$5.75	3.8	3.7	3.5	3.9	4.3	3.8
30lb Washer	$3.50	5.0	4.5	4.2	4.7	5.0	4.6
30lb Dryer	$0.25	28.0	27.2	25.1	27.3	32.6	27.4
50lb Dryer	$0.25	18.2	14.8	14.8	17.6	19.9	16.7
Double	$2.00	2.5	2.0	1.9	2.5	2.4	2.3
Top Loader	$1.50	2.8	2.7	2.6	2.6	2.8	2.7
Wash Turns		3.5	3.2	3.0	3.4	3.6	3.3
Dry Turns		23.1	21.0	20.0	22.5	26.3	22.1

Gas			
$	Units	Cost per unit	% of Gross
$1,177.08	1240	$0.95	10%

Sewer			
$	Units	Cost per unit	% of Gross
$463.32	198	$2.34	4%

Electric			
$	Units	Cost per unit	% of Gross
$453.58	3563	$0.13	4%

Total Utility % of Gross	20.0%
Projected Washer CCF Used	203
Projected Water Expence	$692.41

Water			
$	Units	Cost per unit	% of Gross
$243.54	198	$1.23	2%

Actual Water CCF	198
Actual Water And Sewer Expence	$706.86

With this spreadsheet, we can make a few entries. The top row, titled "days for count," is how many days in each week are in the pull. Then, under the "Week 1" column, we enter how many pounds of quarters we collected for each type of washer and dryer. The spreadsheet does the rest of the work for us, factoring in the number of each machine and the vending price. It then calculates the total gross sales and the number of turns per day.

On the bottom of the table, we can enter our utility expenses at the end of the month and see if it falls within the projected range. In our example, we are at 20 percent of gross income for our utility expense.

I also have a page 2 of this table, which I have not included. In that spreadsheet, I enter in how much water each washer uses and the program projects the water usage and water expense at the end of the month. I take a couple minutes to enter this information at the end of each week and it allows me to examine my turns for any given week or month at quick reference.

In some cases, you may find that the owner doesn't record TPD at all. They simply total all the quarters from every washer and dryer and record them as gross sales.

Others just count the money coming out of the change machine, which is what customers use to turn their paper currency into quarters. Owners will fill the change machine with the quarters they collect from their washers and dryers and count the paper money in the change machine as gross sales. However, this is not accurate because it doesn't account for people who simply use the change machine and leave without doing any laundry. Owners who use this method don't really know their gross sales.

Still others don't do any counting at all and go straight to the club, horse track, or casino with the money they collect and make the rest up as they go. These are the people who are likely behind on the bills at their laundromat and are in some financial trouble. Watch out for them.

One reason we want TPD information is to help us project future earnings if we decide to pursue ownership of the laundromat. Has the location had an increase or decrease in turns from year-to-year? Is there one type of machine that isn't getting used as much? Perhaps some machines need to be replaced if they are not producing enough revenue.

Another way this information is useful is if we decide to do some time-of-day pricing, which is when we reduce the price of doing a load of laundry at a specific time or day. You may have noticed that some laundromats will offer $1.00 loads on Tuesdays, for example. Knowing TPD information will make it easier to project how many turns we will need at the discounted price to produce more revenue.

We also need to be sure that we are being realistic when we project additional income. We can't just say that we are going to increase gross sales by $2,000 a month. Knowing our TPD helps to determine how much business we need to achieve our goal.

CHAPTER 5
OKAY, YOU FOUND ONE. NOW WHAT?

Let's say you've found a laundromat that looks promising and you're wondering what to do next. The owner is telling you all about the money he or she is making. It might look like a great deal, but how can you be sure?

The first step is to verify everything the laundry owner is telling you. After all, it's a cash business, so how do you know that what they are saying is the truth?

The primary goal is to find out if the asking price is reasonable and if the place has cash flow. There are many different philosophies on what a laundry is worth, but we must first find out the essential information. We do that by asking lots of questions.

There isn't an exact science as to which questions to ask, but it's important to get an idea of where the owner's numbers are coming from to make sure they're reliable. In my first communication with an owner, I'll ask a few basic questions. These include:

- *What's the address?*
- *What are your gross sales?*
- *What's your net income?*
- *Why are you selling?*

I then look at the laundromat to see if I am even interested. If so, I call back and ask to set up a meeting, which I prefer to do in person. I ask them to go through the numbers and see what financial information they can share. Some sellers will only give you gross sales numbers and expenses at first and you may have to show additional interest after the first meeting to get more information. This is okay. You'll end up getting more information if you work at their pace.

These are some of the questions you should be asking, some of which you may have already asked:

What is your asking price? How long have you owned this business? Do you rent or do you own?

If they own the building you will want to get specifics on it.

Are there any other units? If so, what is the rental income? What are your taxes, insurance, and maintenance costs? If they rent, what is the rent? How much time is left on your lease? Is that a gross lease or a triple-net lease? How much of your rent is your triple net expense? Do you track your turns? If so, what are they on each type of machine?

After these questions, you'll quickly find out which type of owner you have. In a perfect scenario, the owner will be knowledgeable and have all the necessary information you need. However, you'll find some owners who don't seem to know much of anything. Be careful with these people, but don't rule them out. The business might still be a good one, but you'll need to double-check everything to make sure you're not getting into a bad situation.

Let's continue with the questions.

What are your gross washer and dryer sales? What are your gross vending sales (if applicable)?

Most laundries will only have washer, dryer, and vending as

income. Some will have more. If there are more income streams, we need to ask additional questions:

- *What is your ATM machine income?*
- *What is your video game income?*
- *What is your dry clean revenue?*
- *What is your drop laundry revenue?*
- *What is your tanning revenue?*
- *What are your gross sales from all the laundry bags, detergents, and tanning lotions that you sell over the counter?*
- *Do you have any commercial accounts? What are those sales?*

Once we have all of the revenue information, we need to talk about expenses. The table below is a profit and loss statement, which lists about all of the expenses a common unattended laundromat will have. I use a statement like this one as my pro-forma to project monthly and yearly income and expenses. It is important to fill in all of the numbers we receive from the laundry owner to determine the cash flow of the business.

Pro-Forma

	January	February	March	April
Income				
Coin Laundry	$9,800.00			
Vending Machines	$800.00			
Gross Profit	$10,600.00	$0.00	$0.00	$0.00
Cost of Goods Sold				
Vending Products	$350.00			
Total Cost of Goods Sold	$350.00	$0.00	$0.00	$0.00
Expense				
Education	$0.00			
Advertising and Promotion	$200.00			
Automobile Expense	$0.00			
Business Licenses and Permits	$25.00			
Computer and Internet Expenses	$55.00			
Dues and Subscriptions	$12.00			
Insurance Expense				
General Liability Insurance	$200.00			
Total Insurance Expense	$200.00	$0.00	$0.00	$0.00

Interest Expense	$0.00			
Janitorial Expense	$35.00			
Miscellaneous Expense	$0.00			
Payroll Expenses	$350.00			
Professional Fees	$0.00			
Rent Expense	$1,800.00			
Repairs and Maintenance				
Laundry Maintenance	$175.00			
Repairs and Maintenance - Other	$50.00			
Total Repairs and Maintenance	$225.00	$0.00	$0.00	$0.00
Security Expense	$24.00			
Telephone Expense	$55.00			
Trash Pick-Up	$90.00			
Utilities				
Electric Charges	$425.00			
Gas Charges	$900.00			
Water Charges	$640.00			
Total Utilities	$1,965.00	$0.00	$0.00	$0.00
Debt Service	$1,500.00			
Debt Service	$750.00			
Debt Service	$0.00			
Security Deposits	$0.00			
Total Expense	$7,636.00	$0.00	$0.00	$0.00
Net Ordinary Income	$2,964.00	$0.00	$0.00	$0.00

I have included some lines on the tables that you may not need. For example, I believe every laundry should have security cameras that are viewable over the Internet. Therefore, you'll need an Internet connection. Subscriptions would include a daily newspaper or magazines.

I included payroll because you may not want to personally clean your laundromat every day, so you might need a cleaning service or an employee to clean it for you. You might also want to have someone there during busy hours to assist customers. This is common in some neighborhoods where you may need someone there to help keep the peace.

Remember, we must double-check all of these numbers eventually, but to start we are going to use the numbers that the owner gave us. Later, we can change them if needed.

If it is an attended laundry with other services, the pro-forma may look like the following page:

Pro-Forma

	January	February	March	April
Income				
Commercial Accts	$300.00			
Internet	$125.00			
Coin Laundry	$16,000.00			
Wash & Fold	$600.00			
Dry Cleaning	$450.00			
Over The Counter Sales	$250.00			
Tanning Packages	$700.00			
Vending Machines	$1,050.00			
Gross Profit	$19,475.00	$0.00	$0.00	$0.00
Cost of Goods Sold				
Dry Cleaning Expense	$295.00			
Merchant Account Fees	$36.00			
Over the counter sales	$65.00			
Vending Products	$450.00			
Total Cost of Goods Sold	$846.00	$0.00	$0.00	$0.00
Expense				
Education	$100.00			
Advertising and Promotion	$840.00			
Automobile Expense	$140.00			
Business Licenses and Permits	$25.00			
Cash Drawer Payouts	$250.00			
Chartible Contributions	$50.00			
Computer and Internet Expenses	$100.00			
Wash & Fold Supplies	$75.00			
Dues and Subscriptions	$70.00			
Insurance Expense				
General Liability Insurance	$200.00			
Tan Insurance	$150.00			
Worker's Compensation	$150.00			
Total Insurance Expense	$500.00	$0.00	$0.00	$0.00
Interest Expense	$0.00			
Janitorial Expense	$50.00			
Meals and Entertainment	$0.00			
Laundry Supplies	$56.00			
Miscellaneous Expense	$75.00			
Office Supplies	$65.00			
Payroll Expenses	$1,600.00			
Postage and Delivery	$12.00			
Professional Fees	$0.00			
Reconciliation Discrepancies	$0.00			
Rent Expense	$2,900.00			
Repairs and Maintenance				
Laundry Maintenance	$200.00			
Tanning Maintenance	$50.00			
Repairs and Maintenance - Other	$75.00			
Total Repairs and Maintenance	$325.00	$0.00	$0.00	$0.00
Security Expense	$66.00			
Small Tools and Equipment	$60.00			
Tanning Supplies	$5.00			
Telephone Expense	$185.00			

Trash Pick-Up	$90.00			
Utilities				
Electric Charges	$726.00			
Gas Charges	$1,500.00			
Water Charges	$900.00			
Total Utilities	$3,126.00	$0.00	$0.00	$0.00
Debt Service	$1,700.00			
Debt Service	$800.00			
Debt Service	$0.00			
Total Expense	$14,111.00	$0.00	$0.00	$0.00
Net Ordinary Income	$5,364.00	$0.00	$0.00	$0.00

When filling in the pro-forma, we need to examine and prove each number. If the seller says he is paying $200 per month for insurance, we need proof. I always ask for a copy of his insurance policy with the offer and then make some phone calls to see if I can get a better rate.

If his payroll is $1,600, we need to break that down. How many employees does he have, how many hours do they work, and what does each of them get paid? If the seller states that he has $600 per month in drop laundry sales, we need to see the cash register slips or invoices that back that number.

Keep in mind that if we are serious about buying this business, we will eventually need to make an offer. With that offer we are going to ask for the business's last three years of P&L statements, income taxes, utility information, and more. However, for now we just want to know if the place makes any money, based on what the owner has told us.

Going back to your interview, ask about specific numbers. For example, let's say the owner tells you that he or she gets five turns per day on the washers. Your first question should be, "Is that for your tops or triple-loaders?"

The owner's answer might be something like: "I do five turns per day on my triples, three on my tops, and four on my doubles. I gross about $9,000 a month on my washers. I don't track my dryers' TPD, but I gross about $4,000 a month."

How do you know if this all adds up? Some quick math comes in handy.

When you were at the laundromat before your meeting, you would have written down the vending prices of each type of washer and dryer. You would have also counted how many of each type of machine there were. (If you were really diligent, you would have also gotten model numbers, usually located on the back of the washers.)

In our example, you counted that the laundry had 12 top loaders, eight double loaders, and six triple loaders. It also had 10 stack dryers, for a total of 20 dryer pockets.

Let's do the math:

- *12 top loaders at $1.50 each and 3 TPD = $54/day x 30 days = $1,620 per month*
- *8 doubles at $2.25 each and 4 TPD = $72/day x 30 days = $2,160 per month*
- *6 triples at $3.50 each and 5 TPD = $105/day x 30 days = $3,150 per month*

If the owner gave us the correct turns, the gross sales number for the washers should be about $6,930 per month. However, from our conversation with the owner, we were told that the gross was $9,000. In this situation, the numbers don't add up. Believe it or not, this is a common occurrence.

Dryer revenue is a little harder to figure out. Usually, it's anywhere from 35 to 55 percent of the wash revenue, depending on the dryer vending price. At my laundromat I average about 54 percent, which I calculate by dividing my dryer revenue by my washer revenue.

In our scenario, the owner stated that the dryer revenue was $4,000. If we take $4,000/$9,000, we get 44 percent, so we'll work with that number.

Another number in the pro-forma that may vary is utility expense. This can run anywhere between 13 to 30 percent of the washer and dryer revenue. There are many factors involved, such as the price of natural gas and the age of the equipment. It all depends on the location.

Below I have included a spreadsheet that displays water usage, which is also available on my website:

Forecast by Turns & Water Usage

	A	B	C	D	E	F	G
	Washers	# of Washers	Vend Price	Turns per day	Daily Total	Monthly Total	Annual Total
1	Top Loaders	12	$1.50	3	$54.00	$1,620.00	$19,440.00
2	Water Usage Per	35					
3	Total Gal / CCF	37800	51				
4	Doubles	8	$2.25	4	$72.00	$2,160.00	$25,920.00
5	Water Usage Per	15					
6	Total Gal / CCF	14400	19				
7	25lb	0	$2.25	0	$0.00	$0.00	$0.00
8	Water Usage Per	50					
9	Total Gal / CCF	0	0				
10	30lb	0	$3.25	0	$0.00	$0.00	$0.00
11	Water Usage Per	95					
12	Total Gal / CCF	0	0				
13	35lb	6	$3.50	5	$105.00	$3,150.00	$37,806.00
14	Water Usage Per	95					
15	Total Gal / CCF	85500	114				
16	40lb	0	$4.00	0	$0.00	$0.00	$0.00
17	Water Usage Per	100					
18	Total Gal / CCF	0	0				
19	50lb	0	$4.50	0	$0.00	$0.00	$0.00
20	Water Usage Per	115					
21	Total Gal / CCF	0	0				
22	60lb	0	$5.50	0	$0.00	$0.00	$0.00
23	Water Usage Per	125					
24	Total Gal / CCF	0	0				
25	80lb	0	$6.75	0	$0.00	$0.00	$0.00
26	Water Usage Per	150					
27	Total Gal / CCF	0	0				

		# of Dryers	Vend Price	Turns per day	Daily Total	Monthly Total	Annual Total
28	Dryers						
29	30lb	20	$0.25	21	$105.00	$3,150.00	$37,800.00
30	Minutes	10					
31	50lb	0	$0.00	0	$0.00	$0.00	$0.00
32	Minutes	8					
33	Washer Income			Dryer / Washer	45.45%	$6,930.00	$83,160.00
34	Dryer Income			Percentage		$3,150.00	$37,800.00
35	Monthly Income					$10,080.00	
36	Annual Income						$120,960.00
37	Water Usage	Billed	Washer Usage				
38	Month	1	1				
39	CCF	0	184				
40	Gallons	0	137700				
	A	B	C	D	E	F	G

Take a moment to become familiar with this spreadsheet. Section 1A, which reads "top loaders," can be changed to any type of washer you have. In section 1B, we enter the number of washers that we have and in 1C we enter the vending price of that washer. The projected number of turns goes in section 1D, and in 2B we enter how much water that washer uses in one load.

When using this sheet, you'll notice that the whenever you change one of the variables, it automatically calculates totals in sections 1E, 1F, 1G, and 3B. All of the totals will then recalculate at the bottom of the table.

Let's say you want to see what happens to your gross if you increase your turns on your top loaders from 3 to 4, and perhaps you want to increase your vending price by a quarter. Or, maybe you'd like to add another washer. To make a projection, simply enter the new numbers into the spreadsheet (in the white boxes) and see what happens. The table is set up so that every type of washer calculates in the same way.

This sheet also works for dryers, so change any variable in the white boxes and check the totals. If you change the dryer minutes, you will have to manually change the turns to reflect that change. Each quarter equals one turn.

If you look at sections 33F, 33G, 34F, and 34G, you'll see the monthly and annual totals for the washers and dryers. In 33E, the washer and dryer revenue percentage changes automatically when any income-producing variable is changed.

When it comes to water usage, we want to enter the correct amount of each machine, like in section 2B. This will give us a total number of gallons and CCFs used with our projected turns or revenue targets. If you change the water usage in 2B, you'll notice the totals in 3B and 3C also change.

Once all of the washers and turns are figured correctly, we can look at sections 39C and 40C for our water usage totals. In 39B and 40B, we enter the totals directly from the water bill so we can see how close we are to the actual water use for this particular laundromat.

You might notice that there are some water usage assumptions in the table, like the fact that the double loader only uses 15 gallons of water (section 5B). In this example, I am assuming that the owner has a high-efficiency washer.

Determining water usage is generally easier with older machines than it is with newer ones. This is mainly because old machines use a set amount of water each time, while newer machines can be programmed to use different amounts within a certain range, which can be quite a few gallons' difference. You may need to find out at which setting the washer is programmed and then call the manufacturer to figure out the amount of gallons used at that setting.

You can also visit www.irs.gov/pub/irs-mssp/laundry. pdf and see how the IRS audits laundromats, backing in off of a water bill and using certain usage assumptions. It's an interesting read.

This is another situation in which having a knowledgeable owner makes a big difference, so it doesn't hurt to ask. See if you can get hold of a water bill and look at the overall usage for the location.

The Internet is another valuable tool in this effort. In my municipality, for example, there is a web page where I can enter in an address and I can find the water bill for that location. I would suggest searching the Web for your water works department and if they don't have the information posted online, give them a call. They will release more information than you'd think.

To successfully use the water bill information, you'll need to know the billing cycle. Where I'm at, we get billed every three months. So naturally, I take the total usage on the bill and divide by three. Then I break it down into gallons and enter them into my spreadsheet in section 39B.

Often times, water use is measured in Centum Cubic Feet (CCF) or Hundred Cubic Feet (HCF). One CCF or HCF is equal to 748 gallons, which is how this spreadsheet is figured.

Once we know the number of gallons the laundromat has used, we can enter those numbers into the TPD spreadsheet. Then we can compare our assumptions with actual usage data. It won't be exact, but it provides for a close estimate.

• • •

As previously stated, the spreadsheet is set up for many different types of equipment. We can change any variable that is boxed in and the spreadsheet (in Microsoft Excel) will calculate the rest. The first entry is the number of top load washers with the gallons per load listed directly underneath. To find this out, I called the manufacturer and gave them the model number. They said that the model uses about 35 gallons per load.

After that, we can enter the vending price and TPD, and the spreadsheet will calculate the revenue based on entries. Continue this process with each type of washer.

Here is where we may need to go back and ask some more questions. Remember how, based on the turns the owner gave us, we came up with a lower monthly income? The owner said the gross was $9,000 per month on his washers, but we figured about $6,930 (33F) with the turn information we received.

We can use this spreadsheet to increase the turns until we get to the amount the owner gave us. On the following table, we're going to go back and examine the turns.

Forecast by Turns & Water Usage

	A	B	C	D	E	F	G
	Washers	# of Washers	Vend Price	Turns per day	Daily Total	Monthly Total	Annual Total
1	Top Loaders	12	$1.50	4.5	$81.00	$2,430.00	$29,160.00
2	Water Usage Per	35					
3	Total Gal / CCF	56700	76				
4	Doubles	8	$2.25	5.2	$93.60	$2,808.00	$33,696.00
5	Water Usage Per	15					
6	Total Gal / CCF	18720	25				
7	25lb	0	$2.25	0	$0.00	$0.00	$0.00
8	Water Usage Per	50					
9	Total Gal / CCF	0	0				
10	30lb	0	$3.25	0	$0.00	$0.00	$0.00
11	Water Usage Per	95					
12	Total Gal / CCF	0	0				
13	35lb	6	$3.50	6	$126.00	$3,780.00	$45,360.00
14	Water Usage Per	95					
15	Total Gal / CCF	102600	137				
16	40lb	0	$4.00	0	$0.00	$0.00	$0.00
17	Water Usage Per	100					
18	Total Gal / CCF	0	0				
19	50lb	0	$4.50	0	$0.00	$0.00	$0.00
20	Water Usage Per	115					
21	Total Gal / CCF	0	0				

	A	B	C	D	E	F	G
22	60lb	0	$5.50	0	$0.00	$0.00	$0.00
23	Water Usage Per	125					
24	Total Gal / CCF	0	0				
25	80lb	0	$6.75	0	$0.00	$0.00	$0.00
26	Water Usage Per	150					
27	Total Gal / CCF	0	0				
28	Dryers	# of Dryers	Vend Price	Turns per day	Daily Total	Monthly Total	Annual Total
29	30lb	20	$0.25	27	$135.00	$4,050.00	$48,600.00
30	Minutes	10					
31	50lb	0	$0.00	0	$0.00	$0.00	$0.00
32	Minutes	8					
33	Washer Income		Dryer / Washer	44.91%	$9,018.00	$108,216.00	
34	Dryer Income		Percentage		$4,050.00	$48,600.00	
35	Monthly Income					$13,068.00	
36	Annual Income						$156,816.00
37	Water Usage	Billed	Washer Usage				
38	Month	1	1				
39	CCF	0	238				
40	Gallons	0	178020				

From the spreadsheet, we can tell that in order to reach a revenue of $9,000 (33F) from the washers, the turns would have to be increased to 4.5 (1D) on the tops, 5.2 (4D) on the doubles, and six (13D) on the triples. These numbers are between one and 1.5 turns higher than the ones the owner gave us, which is considerable.

To investigate further, we may have to go do some laundry at the location on the weekend and manually count the turns. Weekends tend to be busier than weekdays, so the turns should really be hopping.

We will also want to take a look at the water usage, as it jumped up to 178,020 gallons (238 CCF) (40C) with our new TPD numbers. Remember, at the TPD we were provided, usage was at 137,700 gallons (184 CCF), as seen on the first sheet. That's a big difference.

Perhaps the owner doesn't know how to calculate TPD, so we definitely need to see a water bill to check the actual usage to give us a better idea of gross sales. If we get a quarterly water bill and the usage is close to 552 CCF (184 x 3), then we know the gross is closer to the lower number. However, if it's closer to 714 CCF (238 x 3), then his gross may be closer to the higher number.

I certainly don't want to assume that the gross is $9,000 when it actually is closer to the $6,930 we got from the TPD that he supplied. Again, this is no exact science, so don't rely solely on this spreadsheet. Use your own judgment, but this table serves as another tool in your tool box.

Another thing to keep in mind is that water usage bills will also include toilets, sinks, and possibly other storefronts that could increase usage. Your water works department will have assumptions for public toilets and sinks and you need to subtract for those when crunching the numbers.

We want to know the exact amount of water the laundromat uses each month. To do this, we might need to look at the owner's records to see the exact revenue he collected. This is where the fun begins. It's never easy going over someone's poorly kept records.

• • •

Let's say that, taking everything into account, you are still interested in the business. The numbers look good and you think that the place will generate cash flow for you.

You're still at the point where you need to do a little more research.

First off, it's a good idea to know exactly who owns the property. Depending on your municipality, you may be able to find this online. In my city, it's all on the city assessor's web page. From here you can also see what the tax bill is and if it was paid. This is all public information and if your city doesn't post it online, you can call and they will give it to you over the phone.

In a situation where you'll be leasing the space, you'll want to find information about the landlord. If you're buying the property, you'll need to know if the taxes are up to date, or you will be the one responsible if you close on the deal.

I was looking at a laundromat a few months back and the owner of the property was three years behind on his taxes. The tenants of the building were in a triple-net lease and were paying for a portion of the taxes, but the owner wasn't. After further investigation, I found that the owner was causing all kinds of trouble and filing lawsuits against the city for some other properties he owned. I also found out that the city had bulldozed one of his properties for code violations. Knowing I didn't want to get involved in a mess like that, I passed.

You can also look up the seller's personal property tax for equipment. Again, this is public information and you have a right to know if he or she is behind with the city.

If you don't want to wait for the owner to provide the gas and electric invoices, you may also call the utility. Some of this information is private, but they will usually share averages with you.

Another note regarding gas and electric bills is that in some areas they charge a security deposit. Where I live, it's equal to two of the highest monthly bills in the last 24 months, which could be thousands. Because of this, it's a good idea to call and see if they have a security deposit and how much it would be for that location.

With some businesses, you need to consider every angle, including finding out the age of the equipment. Is everything

15 years or older? At 15 years, you may be pushing your luck, but there is no magic number. I have machines that are over 15 years old and run perfectly, but they do tend to be water hogs and the maintenance is high. Because of that, I'm constantly working on them.

That brings up another point. If you plan on owning a laundromat, it helps to be handy. It will save you a lot of money in the long run.

If the laundromat you're considering has a lot of old equipment, you do have some options other than buying all new machines. There is a ton of equipment out there that may only be a few years old and it just takes is a little effort to find it. Usually this equipment is up for sale because somebody was sold on an idea to build a brand-new laundromat and it failed.

Call the distributors and check CraigsList, eBay, and the trade magazines' classified ads. I actually know people who have built new laundromats using nearly new machines and saved a ton of money.

The point is that you may get a good deal on a laundromat because its equipment is outdated. The basic infrastructure may be there and all you need to do is make some improvements. Some of the best finds are the ones that need a couple pieces of equipment, a good cleaning, paint, new flooring, some ceiling tiles, lights, a fixed-up bathroom, security cameras, and better signage.

• • •

Another research method you should implement is to run a demographic report, although you may need the assistance of a distributor to help you interpret it.

When you do so, you'll find that most of your customers are low-income renters, a population that needs to be in close proximity to your laundromat. Chapter 11 provides more detail on who your customers will be and what you can do to attract them.

Having low income renters doesn't mean your laundromat has to be in a bad neighborhood. College students are a good example of low-income renters who often live in the more desirable parts of town, near a campus.

To run a demographic report, contact the CLA. They can do one for you at a very low cost (if you're a member) and it is a great learning experience. It allows you to learn pretty quickly which location is best for a laundromat.

I first ordered a demographic report in an area that I knew was a great place for a laundromat, as there were several large stores located there. I then ordered another report for an area that I was familiar with, but wasn't a laundry hot spot. I compared the two, looked at the demographics for both, and continued to order reports for locations all over the city.

When you do this, you will begin to see patterns. Some areas are more densely populated, have more renters, and tend to be more low-income. Laundromats tend to thrive in areas with a lot of low-income renters.

After running your report, call the city and make sure they're not going to tear up the street anytime soon. Call the planning commission to make sure no one is proposing any major changes in the area. You might also want to drive around and make sure someone isn't building a new laundromat nearby. This could be the reason your laundry owner wants to sell.

• • •

To end this chapter, I would like to tell you about a recent experience I had that demonstrates the need to have all the facts before purchasing a laundromat.

A few weeks ago, a man walked into my store and started to make small talk. He told me of my laundry's previous owner and started naming a few people he knew in the business.

He mentioned a particular laundromat that I knew of well. The owner had responded to one of my letters of interest and I had checked the place out. He had built the laundry in an existing building 25 years earlier and apparently hadn't done a thing since. It contained almost all top loaders priced super cheap and the owner was making only a few hundred dollars profit per month, which I figured out from my interview and spreadsheets.

His asking price was twice the assessed value of the building in a weak real estate market. I was unable to build value with the laundromat's equipment because it all needed to be replaced. The revenue was almost non-existent.

I noticed the place had a basement, which meant that I would have to build a truss system to support the bigger washers that I would need to install. It wasn't a big location at about 1,500 square feet and I remember thinking that the place would shake off its foundation if I put in a few triple loaders. All of the antique single-pocket dryers needed to be replaced as well.

Even if I tried to install slightly used equipment, it didn't make financial sense to pursue the business because of the high asking price, which he wouldn't budge on.

The guy in my store, on the other hand, had a different

story. He was telling me that all it takes to run a laundromat is to collect money because the doors lock and unlock themselves. He went on to talk about how the owner of the other laundry was so busy making money that he didn't have time to fix the equipment. After all, he said, the business had been there so long that the owner had to be raking it in.

I didn't want to interrupt him as he was telling me all about this successful owner and how to run a laundromat. He seemed pretty full of himself, so I just let him talk. To myself, however, I was thinking about how detached he was from reality.

I knew for a fact that the other owner was making very little money and that the equipment was broken because he couldn't afford to fix it. The place was just a dump.

As the guy in my store kept going on and on, I thought to myself, "What an idiot! How can he possibly think that the other owner is making too much money to fix his equipment? Was he wearing a blindfold when he was in the place? The store didn't even have a working change machine!" It didn't make any sense.

In fact, when the owner was showing me around he was complaining about how the city made him put toilet paper in the bathroom. He also said that he took out the fire extinguishers after city inspections because he thought someone would steal it. He was making no money and it was evident in his water bill.

The moral of the story is that you can't let someone trying to sell a laundromat fill your head with false information. Do your research and find the truth for yourself. The numbers don't lie.

CHAPTER 6
THE WALK-THROUGH

One of the most important things you should do when considering buying a laundromat is to spend time there and make some observations.

Be sure to note your first impression, as this is what a new customer will see. How does the place look? Would you do laundry there? You need to find what the current owner is doing wrong and what you would do to improve it. The more things you can improve upon, the better your chances of doing better than he or she currently is.

Some people have a specific number of improvements they look for during a walk-through. They say that if they can find ten things they can improve, then they're interested. Some of these things are easy, like paint, flooring, indoor signage, working equipment, keeping the laundry clean, better security, advertising, vending price, lack of seating or tables, lack of carts, or better outdoor signage.

Also, you should look for what cannot be improved, like parking, location, a bad lease, or new competition. Some locations just can't be helped.

When it comes to outdoor signage, look to see if what they already have is adequate. Is the sign easily visible from the street? Is it lit up at night?

Front windows are a great spot to stick large vinyl letters, spelling things like "COIN LAUNDRY" or "LAUNDROMAT," or any special pricing for certain days or times. If there are improvements to be made in terms of signage, make some phone calls to get an idea of what an outdoor sign would cost and figure it into the overall cost of purchasing the location.

While walking through the store, make a list of improvements you'll need to make and try to put a dollar value on them. If the ceiling has stains, there are probably water leaks. Have they been fixed? Hopefully there will be some customers there, so watch to see what they are doing. Are they sitting on the tables? Are there enough chairs? Look to see if they have enough clothes folding tables and carts.

Make improvements that will have the greatest impact first. Prioritize your list and keep it for after you close on the business. Your mind will be going a million miles an hour with all the other stuff at that time and you will need this list to keep you on track. It's never too early to begin planning.

In terms of equipment, take a look around to make sure it's all working properly. If there are several "out of order" signs, it may have a "hands off" owner.

In my experience, breakdowns come in waves. Everything may be going great for a few months, but then all of a sudden there's a bearing on a 50 lb. washer, a transmission on a top loader, your changer transport needs maintenance, and the door lock fails on a triple loader. Breakdowns are expensive, but owners need to stay on top of them and fix everything as soon as possible.

When it comes to equipment, there are some things you can look at to see if the machines are going to need attention soon. These inspections should be done before you buy the laundromat, but it's also important to do regular check-ups on your equipment once you take over.

The pieces of information I'm providing are some basic service suggestions. If you have no experience with laundromats you should pay to have a service person come through and inspect everything. These people will have more expertise and will be able to identify a problem much more quickly and accurately.

Let's start with the top load washers. If there's water on the floor, it's probably from a customer who overloaded the machine. It happens a lot. Check all of the water lines, including the supply hoses and drain hose, to make sure it's not the washer itself. It could be something like the drain hose came a little loose.

Belts are a minor maintenance issue. Some top loaders have belts that operate the transmission and the drain pump located on the bottom of the washer, so you'll have to lift up the front to see them. Look to see if they are cracked or have any big chunks missing. They may be glazed over, causing the belt to slip an excessive amount. This is caused by customers overloading the washer to the point of the belt slipping and overheating.

Another tip is to check the damper pads, which keep the washer tub moving side to side freely during the spin cycle. Simply grab the agitator and move it back and forth a little. If it's hard to move or feels like it's grabbing on something, the pads may need to be replaced. If they're not, the washer will go out of balance easily, potentially causing greater problems.

If you notice any grease, oil, or anything else under the washer, you will want to pull off the front panel. Look inside to see if there are any leaks or if it looks like something has been sprayed on the inside walls. If that is the case there may be a bad tub bearing or tub seal.

The larger front load washers ranging from 20 to 80 lbs. have a couple of common issues to look for. First, check the shaft bearings by pulling up on the wash basket. If you have some up-movement on the basket, there may be a bad bearing. This is a very expensive repair and could cost anywhere from a couple hundred dollars to a few thousand, depending on the make, model, and size of the machine. Having several bad bearings will affect the price of the laundromat.

You may also want to inspect the belts on these washers, which could be visible from the rear or when you open the top cover. Look for any water that may be leaking and pay special attention to the supply hoses starting at the water valve and follow them through the washer to the soap dispenser. Is everything connected securely? Is there any water where it shouldn't be?

Pay attention to the area around the washer. Is it dry or wet? Check to see if water is coming out of the drain hose, as some washers drain into a large pit before the water goes down the drain. If the drain hose is visible, is water leaking while the washer is not running? If so, look into it. It may be something simple, like a diaphragm that is inside the water valve.

If the washer is running, do you have water leaking out of the drain hose during the wash cycle? You may have something stuck in the drain valve. Bra wires and credit cards tend to get stuck in there quite often, preventing the drain from closing all the way. If you have a washer acting up, always check the drain valve first, as they seem to be the source of a lot of problems.

Make sure you regularly inspect the door seals. Does the gasket around the door have any tears in it? If the washer is running, listen for any thumping noises or the sound of a motor whining. If you hear something, get it checked by a professional.

Also, can you read the display on the front of the washer? Are the directions for operation beginning to fade or peel off? Are the prices clearly marked? Customers will not use a machine if they don't know how much it costs.

When looking at the dryers, you can check the belts in the rear. You may have to remove the back cover to see them. Also, check the dryer door seals and the display panel and again listen for any noises while they're running.

When it comes to dryer duct work and make-up air, you are going to need a professional opinion. Make-up air is a whole issue on its own. Dryers need a certain amount of fresh air to operate effectively and efficiently and they get it through ducts or vents reaching outside. This airflow needs to be sufficient or it will cause problems down the road. It's not a bad idea to ask the previous owner when the dryer ducts were last cleaned, if ever. If they were never cleaned, it makes for an inefficient dryer and a potential fire hazard.

Open the dryer's front panel and look inside. Is everything covered in lint? Are the lint traps clean? How often have they been cleaned? If they have an inch of lint, I would say that they haven't been cleaned in a while.

There may be some additional maintenance that needs to be done to clean up the dryers. Once a year I pull off the front and rear covers (and in some cases pull out the whole burner unit) and vacuum everything. Everything will be covered in lint. The dryer will run better, be more efficient and less of a fire hazard if it's clean. I have had fires, so this is important.

Bill changers need a lot of attention and you'll want to make sure they're updated to accept all of the most recent changes in paper currency. The Federal Reserve is making more and more changes to paper bills to help reduce counterfeiting and will continue to do so for years to come. Older changers may not be able to be updated. If that is the case, make some phone calls to see what a new changer will run you, but I must warn you that they can be expensive.

Changers have front load and rear load cabinets. I like the rear load best because you will be out of the customers' view when you're filling the changers with quarters. If you have to service the changer, it's nice to dump out the quarters in privacy. I don't like people standing over my shoulder when it comes to money.

While you're in the laundromat, get some change to make sure the changer works. Take the change and get a soda, some chips, and a vend-size box of soap. That way you can see if the vending machines are working properly.

Finally, water heaters are expensive to replace and can account for about half of your gas bill during the summer. Have a technician check over the water heater to see if it's in good working condition. If it is a tank system, is the water tank insulated? Newer units are much more efficient and can reduce your water heating expense significantly.

There are also tankless water heaters now that only heat on demand. They can be very efficient, but can be expensive to retrofit into your application. Some of the new water heaters are nearly 100 percent efficient and can also save you big on gas bills. Consult with a distributor to see if this is an option.

After taking a close look around the place and coming up with a list of improvements, factor in the projected cost of those improvements into the total cost of the laundromat. Is it still worth buying?

CHAPTER 7
WHAT'S IT WORTH?

There are many different philosophies on how to determine what a laundromat is worth. To be honest, I'm not exactly sure which are right or wrong, but every seller seems to know exactly what his or her store is worth, or so they think.

How do you decide? Let me run two scenarios past you involving potential laundromats and we'll see what you think. These are based on my experiences.

SCENARIO#1

I was looking at a laundromat that was for sale. It was about 2,000 square feet and had a nice mix of washers and dryers. It had eight top loaders, 10 double loaders, six triple loaders, four 50 lb. washers, two 80 lb. washers, and 15 stack dryers (for a total of 30 dryer pockets).

All of the equipment in the place was about five years old, except for the two 80 lb. washers, which the owner told me he had purchased three years earlier. Several machines had "out of order" signs, but I knew that I could probably fix them myself and figured I could get at least another 10 to 12 years out of the equipment.

The laundry was being sold by the original owner, who had built the place five years earlier. He was going on and on about how great the equipment was and how he personally oversaw everything while it was being built. He even said that the inspectors commented on how nice everything was and that the contractors did quality work. It was a little overkill on the sales pitch, but I listened.

Outside, parking was limited to four spaces, although the place would have been crowded with four families inside. The owner was leasing the building with reasonable rent and was locked into that rate for the next 10 years.

The laundry itself looked neglected. There were signs of vandalism and the place was dimly lit. It needed better signage, security cameras, and some new drywall. But, for about $5,000 to $10,000, I thought I could get it back in top shape.

While I was interviewing the owner, he told me that the business made about $5,500 to $6,000 per month in gross sales, but he had no idea what his TPD were. He said that his expenses were in check, so the laundromat made him about $1,500 per month in profit. I knew that the number wasn't great, but I also knew that I could make improvements and do better.

I conducted a pro-forma with his numbers and they didn't pan out for me. He wanted $140,000 for the place, so I figured that with a loan and a lot of cash down, I would only be making about $300 to $500 per month. I wanted to see if he had more revenue, so I asked to see some of his records to verify the laundry's income.

Everything he had recorded was written on scrap pieces of paper, including numbers from the past three years. He wouldn't let me make any copies of the records and would only let me look at them from a distance, but I could see weekly and monthly totals. The totals showed me that he usually grossed about $3,500 each month, and only a couple times made as much as $5,000.

Obviously, this contradicted what he had told me, so I did some research by pulling his water bill. I was able to figure out that he was averaging less than one turn per day on most of his equipment. I knew that I could do better, but the real question was how this person was doing so poorly. The demographics of the location were promising and the nearest competition was two miles away.

So what was it worth?

SCENARIO #2

Around that very same time, another laundry came up for sale on the other end of town. It was about 2,200 square feet and had about the same laundry capacity as the laundromat described in Scenario #1.

The mix of equipment was a little different, as it had 18 top loaders, eight double loaders, eight triple loaders, and four 50 lb. washers. For dryers, it had ten 30 lb. stacks (20 dryer pockets) and four 50 lb. single stack pocket dryers. The equipment was mostly older stuff, around 15-17 years old and looking beat. However, the 50 lb. washers were only about five years old.

Parking at this location was limited and you could see two other laundromats from the front door. I drove around and found a couple of brand-new laundromats within a mile. The demographics of this location were very strong, which was why there were probably so many competitors.

According to the owner, this laundromat grossed about $11,200 per month, although revenue had been decreasing over the last few years. Rent was a little high, but the lease had two five-year options locked in with minimal increases. The owner's net profit was about $3,000 per month before debt service. While it wasn't a business you could retire on, it was worth looking into. I researched the water bill and the numbers the owner gave me were accurate.

The laundromat also needed some cosmetic work, including new paint, lights, and flooring, but the main concern was equipment. Machines are expensive and this stuff was old and looked rough. Maybe, I thought, I could go with a new/used mix to save some money.

Anyway, he wanted $110,000. What was it worth?

• • •

The first owner was telling me that the equipment was worth at least $140,000. That's taking into account that he paid over $250,000 about five years ago, so he said it was a pretty good deal. The second owner had some older machines, but said that the place was running itself and required minimal upkeep. Basically, the sales pitch was that it was free money.

Some people, when making a purchase like this, use gross income to reach a selling price. Others base it on the assets. Still others do combination of both. However, the approach I like best is based on a multiple of the net income.

Essentially, I don't care what the laundromat grosses, but rather the net income. A laundromat could gross a quarter of a million dollars a year and still lose money if its expenses are not in line. So, I take the laundromat's net annual income and multiply it by a number between one and five, based on other factors like the lease situation, location, equipment, parking, demographics, what work needs to be done, and the overall appearance. The better these factors at the start, the higher the multiplier I use of the net income.

There is no exact rule of thumb for this, but generally I will pay more for a laundry if it has a good location, looks nice, and needs less work. If the equipment is newer and the lease is good, I'll bump up the multiplier. If the place makes a ton of money but needs new equipment, I take that into consideration and subtract a little from the multiplier. If there is a bad lease, I multiply by zero. I have heard many horror stories, so my advice is to stay away from those situations.

The first owner was right in that if I were to build a new laundromat with his used equipment, I would pay about $140,000 for it. However, if I sold the equipment at a going out of business sale, it would probably only be worth about $50,000, perhaps less. It helps to make an asset list for each location and put values on all of the equipment involved.

At the first laundromat, the annual net income was probably around $15,000, after everything was considered. However, the equipment was nice and I would have liked to have a nice laundromat with newer machines. The problem was that the place just didn't make any money. After my loan, I would have anywhere from a loss to maybe a few hundred dollars profit. I would have to do a lot more business to have any success there.

Because the owner was asking for $140,000, the asking price was over nine times the net income. That was well over my maximum multiplier of five, which would have resulted in a $75,000 price tag. All things considered, even that was too much for a place like this.

I explained the multiplier method and told him that I would only be interested if the price went down to around

$50,000. He was angry, but I think he knew where I was coming from. We never did make a deal and the place is looking pretty bad right now. It was vandalized again and all of the top loaders are out of order. I may approach him again soon, but unfortunately for him, the worse the place looks the less my offer will be.

The second laundromat, on the other hand, made some good money for a smaller place. At a net income multiplier of one I was at $36,000 and at a multiplier of five I was looking at $180,000. This site was more promising, as the asking price of $110,000 was within that range.

However, I had a tough decision because I didn't know how long this location would continue to make money. Competition was only going to get worse and the laundromat needed new equipment soon. I had to ask myself what my loan would be with new equipment and if I was going to make any profit with it hanging over me. On top of that, if another laundromat popped up in the area, I would be toast.

When I looked at the numbers, I noticed that the revenue had been decreasing over the past few years. Was it the competition around the location taking up more of the market share? There were too many questions and I never did make an offer because it seemed like a losing proposition. The laundries around it were too big and doing too well. I probably wouldn't have been able to compete for long.

By now you might think I'm crazy. After all, I just passed on a laundromat that was profitable and made an offer on one that was losing money.

Let me tell you that there was sound reasoning behind my decision. The second laundromat was being run very well, even though the equipment was beat. The owner was making as much money as he could with his equipment and nearby competition, it was only going to get worse for him.

The first laundromat, on the other hand, was not being run at all. The owner didn't want anything to do with the place, which was obvious when I walked through the door. All he did was collect money, as he apparently thought that laundry was a hands-off business. Unfortunately, that's not the case. Just like any other small business, it takes a lot of work to stay competitive and successful.

Run-down places tend to attract a very shady clientele, which turns off good customers. Between that and the machines not working, it was hard for the owner to keep people coming. However, I knew that I could turn a place like that around, if it was worth my time and money. By cleaning the place up, advertising, promotional pricing, and a grand re-opening event, I could create some great local buzz for the establishment.

As you are looking at laundromats, don't be afraid to ask how they came up with the selling price. Some owners have simply pulled a number out of thin air, but most have some kind of rationale behind it. It seems that most people go off of assets alone, so we must educate the seller.

For example, if we have two auto parts stores across the street from each other and they both have the same inventory, building type, parking, and signage, it's hard to tell what each is worth based on assets. But, if we learn that one nets $125,000 a year and the other nets $25,000, it becomes obvious which one is worth more. So we can't make decisions based on assets alone.

A factor to keep in mind when looking at any business is

cash flow. No matter what the price of the business, you need to make money on it. Your down payment, of course, is going to affect cash flow. Also, in many cases you may agree on a selling price, but when you figure in your loan payment on the pro-forma, it just doesn't make financial sense. It helps to work on creative financing, but don't overstretch yourself. Make sure the numbers work.

This relates back to the importance of the pro-forma. Some people may be able to work out a deal with a small percentage down by raising private funds. That's great, as long as the business still makes money each and every month. However, it also needs to make enough money to cover the unexpected, like those big expenses that always seem to come at the worst time.

This should go without saying, but remember that you need to pay yourself, even if you already have a full-time job and this is just an investment for you. You're probably going to be at this laundromat at least once per day. Your time is worth something.

When considering cash flow, you'll need to figure out how many TPD you'll need to break even. Be realistic with this number. If you need five TPD, you may be looking at the wrong business. Some owners use between two and 2.5 as a break-even number. Depending on the laundromat, that may be high or low.

Once you know how many TPD the laundry currently runs, you can make a good projection based on that knowledge. Don't expect to jump in there and double the turns and make a boatload of cash. Be reasonable and project modest gains over a period of time.

One thing I learned as a landlord in the real estate business is how to project and manage cash flow. Part of the recent real estate collapse has had to do with undercapitalized landlords. People I know were buying properties with no cash down and paying top dollar. Then they would put a second mortgage on the first property to buy a second. They would have some agent telling them that it was a great deal and that with all the appreciation, they could sell in a couple years a make a huge profit.

There were a lot of smart people buying properties with negative cash flows, expecting that they would sell it off and make a ton of money. When many of these people did a pro-forma on a property, they never factored in the water bill, maintenance, and vacancies. Some never even did a pro-forma in the first place. They just thought that if they could buy a property with little to no cash down, it was a good deal. Others actually put a good percentage down but the price was so high that it never made money. Then, when they added the second mortgage, they were only digging themselves into a deeper hole.

That's why I don't buy any property unless the place makes money from day one. If you were one of the lucky few who got in early enough, it may have worked out, but for those who came in at the end when it was popular, it was disastrous.

I was buying rental properties when it was popular as well. However, I sent out letters of interest and simply asked if they wanted to sell. The phone started ringing and I was able to buy some properties below market value by avoiding the agent's commission. Some owners sold at a good price just to get out from under the property. Whatever the reason, I got some great deals.

There is a lot we can learn from other people's mistakes. Right now, thousands of landlords are stuck with properties that are losing money each month and are facing foreclosure.

My point is that the laundromat you're looking at needs to make money. You need to make sure that whatever the selling price may be, it needs to be profitable from day one. This is why the pro-forma is such a crucial piece of the puzzle. It allows you to go high on the expenses and low on the revenue, which gives you a conservative estimate on how much money you'll make.

The most important thing is to be cautious when projecting future income. Make sure you have plenty of cash left over after covering your debts. The unexpected will happen, so plan for it.

If you think you can do better than the current owner, use the turns and water usage worksheets to project more TPD on your washers to see where that puts you income-wise. Remember to be realistic and don't project too great of an increase. Have a plan for how you will reach your goals.

CHAPTER 8
WRITING AN OFFER

Before we begin this chapter, please note that in order to cover all your bases, you'll need an attorney to help you with writing an offer. If you're thinking about going at it alone, I would advise against it. There are just too many little things to worry about that could cost you a small fortune if overlooked. This section of the book is meant to provide you with the basics of developing your offer.

Before you dive in head-first, try to get most of the issues worked out. You don't want to be going back and forth through attorneys with counter offers, as that can get quite expensive. It's best to have a verbal agreement and most of the details worked out before you get the lawyers involved.

When writing an offer, you want to have a back door in case you find something that isn't acceptable and you need to get out of the contract. These are called contingencies and they should be built into the offer. In addition, each state has its own offer-to-purchase agreements, which you will have to draft line by line with your attorney. Earnest money will accompany the offer and it must be written so that it is refundable if contingencies are not met.

Here is a list of some of the things you may want to include in the offer:

1. Any closing pro-rations of insurance premiums or property taxes that will need to be listed.
2. A complete inventory and asset list of all the equipment, with approximate values.
3. A lien search to see if any money is owed on the equipment.
4. Copies of any and all leases, including any equipment leases that may exist.
5. Copies of profit and loss statements for the last four years.
6. Copies of balance sheets for the last four years.
7. All business books and records for the last four years.
8. Copies of tax returns for the last four years.
9. Copies of electric, gas, and water utility bills for the last 24 months.
10. Copies of all current licenses and permits.
11. Franchise agreements, if any.
12. All employee records.

The offer is contingent on acceptable financing. If there is to be any seller financing you need to list the terms of that loan. The dollar amount, interest rate, and payback period of the loan should also be included. It's best to get the loan unsecured, but they may want to attach the loan to some asset in the event you don't pay.

You may also want to include that all contingencies need to be satisfied by the buyer's written waiver of each contingency. That way, you are checking them off as you go and there is no confusion as to what has been met and what has not.

I would also include that you have the right to terminate the offer if any discovery is made that would affect the business, such as if any new competition is found. Perhaps someone is building a laundromat down the road or the city is going to tear up the street for the next year and traffic will be detoured around your business. This will affect the price of the laundromat and you may no longer be interested. A back door in the contract can be a major advantage.

In the offer, you should also include a period of time that the previous owner must dedicate to training. This includes going over the day-to-day operations of the business, such as equipment maintenance and marketing techniques. I would also include a warranty for the equipment. You don't want to take ownership, only to find out that the previous owner hadn't been fixing anything since you made the offer.

With that in mind, there may be some problems with the equipment that don't arise until after the closing. I would try to include as much time for a warranty as you can get, such as 60 days. Have the seller list what equipment is and is not working.

The lease for the laundry space is a big part of the offer. Most owners I talk to have suggested locking in a 20-year term. The reasoning behind it is that if you lose your lease you are out of business. Laundromats are not easy to move and the infra-structure cost alone could be between $100,000 and $200,000, including the supply plumbing, drains, electrical, natural gas lines, duck work, flooring, walls, and even the ceiling tiles.

You need to have acceptable terms with the landlord of the building and have a lease ready to sign so you can take it to the closing. If the lease is not acceptable, you need to back out. This contingency should be built into the offer and needs to be clear in the language.

Another thing I like to throw into the offer is to have the coin changers filled with quarters before I take over. Depending on the size of the changers, this can range from $500 to a few thousand dollars. You don't want to open up on your first day to empty change machines, as you know the seller is going to otherwise empty them on the day of the closing.

It's also important to have any spare parts for the equipment available and to have the vending machines filled with at least a week's supply of soda and snacks.

Finally, the last crucial part of the offer must include a no-compete clause. This means that the previous owner cannot turn around and open a competing laundromat nearby.

When compiling these documents, keep a checklist so you can keep track of when you receive them. That way, you'll know exactly what you still need before you close. There's a lot to remember and both you and the seller will probably be a little overwhelmed.

Remember that it's better to be safe than sorry. The first time I went through this process I was up most nights tossing and turning, but I didn't want to forget anything.

• • •

Now that you have all of this important legal information in front of you, it's time to verify that everything the owner told you was correct. Take all of the numbers from the bills he or she has and enter them into a 12-month pro-forma, including the numbers for each month. This will help you get a better picture, as you can project revenue for different times of the year.

You will notice that revenue and expenses vary from month to month. Certain months are great, while others, like December in my area, are awful.

Verify all of the utility bills and make sure they fall in line with the projections. Remember, the utilities will be anywhere from 13 to 30 percent of the gross washer and dryer revenue. Try to look at a month that has no heating or cooling in the bill to get a more accurate number and note that the newer the equipment, the lower the percentage will be. If the laundry has really old equipment, it will likely be on the higher end of the spectrum.

The price of natural gas, electric, and water also play a role in the percentage. You need to over-project on everything, as this is your last chance to find something that may be inconsistent.

Lease negotiations can be difficult. My first time around, I had about 17 pages of legal mumbo-jumbo to dig through. Without an attorney, I would have been lost. Be sure to allow yourself enough time to read through everything carefully.

One more consideration is what type of business entity you are going to have. Again, you will want to consult your attorney and accountant to figure out which will work best for your situation. You may want to be an LLC or a sole proprietor. You will need a business name, which in some cases won't matter because the sign out front just says "Laundromat" or "Coin Laundry." You can always name the business whatever you want and then have a Doing Business As (DBA) for the current name.

In most states you can go to the Department of Financial Institutions website and create your business entity there. I usually start by searching businesses to make sure there isn't one with the same name I want. I fill out the form and pay by credit card, and within a couple weeks I get a confirmation of my new business entity.

Now that I have a business entity I can get an Employer Identification Number (EIN) from the Internal Revenue Service. Go to www.irs.gov and under the business tab look for instructions on how to apply for an EIN. We will need an EIN number to open a checking account in the business's name.

Next, contact your states's Department of Revenue and get a seller's permit number so you can collect and submit sales tax. You will need to know which sales are and are not taxable. The seller of the business will know, but it is smart to double-check. You don't want to get behind in taxes.

As you are reviewing all the information from the seller, take a look at the permits and licenses he or she has. If you have an accepted offer, you need to start getting your permits in line. This is a list of what I had to get:

1. Self-Service Laundromat License
2. Weights and Measures License (for the scale and dryer timers)
3. Certificate of Occupancy
4. Sprinkler Inspection Certificate
5. Food Dealer License (vending machines)
6. Health Services Permit (tanning beds)

Make sure you have all of the permits and licenses your city requires, or they can shut you down.

CHAPTER 9
FINANCING YOUR BUSINESS

Financing a Laundromat can be tricky.

Actually, financing any new business can be tricky, but I believe that a laundromat is tougher than most other businesses. Why is that? Because it's a cash business and some owners don't report all of their income. The seller is often trying to get top dollar for a business that only reports part of its income, which makes things complicated.

As an owner, I recommend reporting all of your income for a few reasons. First it's the law and you don't want to get caught up with the IRS. Second, you are creating a track record and if you decide to sell you want to be able to prove as much income as possible. And third, if you need to go back to the bank to purchase another location or add equipment you will need to prove all your income. It just makes things easier from all angles.

I'm going to just touch the surface on financing because everybody's situation is different.

What types of financing are out there? There are commercial bank loans, including business loans and SBA-backed loans, home equity loans, second mortgages, seller financing, and private money, just to name a few. Bank loans will require more effort on your part and you will definitely need a business plan.

So what is a business plan? Basically, it's going to give the lender a snapshot of the business and demonstrate your understanding of the industry. It's also going to show how you plan to grow the business and finance it. There are several important elements to a business plan, which I summarize below:

1. THE EXECUTIVE SUMMARY

The executive summary will include the mission statement, which briefly explains your business. Other parts of the executive summary include the date business began, names of the current owners and what they do, the number of employees, the location of the business, a summary of the laundry's growth through the years, and a summary of any future plans. Keep it simple and use bullet points, as you'll have a chance to go more in-depth later.

2. MARKET ANALYSIS

The market analysis section should illustrate your knowledge of laundromats. This should include an industry description and outlook, your target market (including demographics), and an evaluation of your competition. The CLA has some great tools to help you with this part, including a laundry customer profile and the Coin Laundry Industry Survey.

You are going to need to know who your customers are. This includes how much money they make, where they live (apartments or houses), their marital status, and whether or not they have kids. How many of them live within a ½ mile, 1 mile, and 1 ½ mile of this laundromat? How much do they spend on laundry weekly, monthly and annually? What percentage of them do you need to break even or show a profit?

Over the past five years, has this demographic been increasing or decreasing in the area? Your demographic report will tell you this information.

- Do you feel you can gain market share from any weak competition? Why?
- List your pricing strategies. Are you a high price leader or a low price leader in your area?
- List any resources used to obtain this information.
- List what type of advertising you are going to use to reach your projections.

3. COMPANY DESCRIPTION

The company description section should include information about the laundromat, as well as the factors you believe will make this business a success. Be sure to list the marketplace needs that you are trying to satisfy, including the ways in which you plan to satisfy those needs using your laundromat. Success factors might include a superior ability to satisfy your customers' needs, safety, security, outstanding personnel, or a key location. Each of these would give your business a competitive advantage.

4. ORGANIZATIONAL STRUCTURE

This section should include your company's organizational structure, details about the ownership of your company, and profiles of your management team.

Who does what in your business? What is their background? What are they responsible for? These may seem like unnecessary questions to answer in a one or two person laundromat, but the people reading your business plan want to know who's in charge.

You should also include ownership information.

Include the legal structure of your business along with the subsequent ownership information it relates to. Have you incorporated your business? If so, is it an LLC, C, or S corporation? Perhaps you have formed a partnership with someone, and if so, is it a general or limited partnership? Maybe you are a sole proprietor.

Important ownership information that should be in your business plan includes the names of owners, the percentage of ownership, and the extent of involvement they will have with the laundromat.

I think you'll agree that one of the strongest factors for success in any business is the ability and track record of its owners or employees. So, tell the bank about your background. Provide resumes with all the usual information in order to sell yourself.

5. SALES AND MARKETING STRATEGIES

Marketing is the process of creating customers and laundry customers may need to be created more often, as they tend to be a fairly transient population. You will need a marketing strategy to reach all of the new movers coming into the area. In this section, define that strategy.

6. DESCRIPTION OF PRODUCT OR SERVICE

You're probably thinking, "It's a laundromat. What do you think my service is?"

I know, sounds stupid. But how are you filling the needs of your customers? If it's a college town, you'll need a lot of single load washers for the students who only have a load or two of clothes. Maybe you have a lot of big families and that

80 lb. washer is going to save your customers money and provide a great value. It could be that you have so many machines your customers can get in and out faster.

Whatever the case may be, describe how your product fits the needs of your customers. You could also list how you differ from the competition. Why are you better than they are? Do you have newer equipment or larger washers and dryers?

7. THE FUNDING REQUEST

This is essentially how much money you need and the terms you are requesting. Are you going to put down 30 percent, have the seller carry 20 percent, and request the remaining 50 percent over five years at a 9 percent interest rate? Disclose all of the terms in this section.

You could also have different projections, such as a best and worst case scenario. Remember, you will have to cover these loans with projected revenue in a later section. If there are going to be any future funding requirements, you will need to list them as well. Maybe after three years you'll want to purchase new dryers. List how much money you will need at that time and how you plan on paying those loans.

8. FINANCIALS

When doing your due diligence on the business, a financial picture should be developed. You now know what the business has done in the past and what you can expect in the future. Your lender is going to want the same information. The following are the financial statements that should be included in your business plan packet:

HISTORICAL FINANCIALS

You are buying an established business, so you will be requested to supply historical data related to the laundromat's performance. Most creditors request data for the last three to five years, depending on the length of time they have been in business.

The historical financial data you would want to include would be the laundromat's income statements, balance sheets, and cash flow statements for each year. Often, creditors are also interested in any collateral you may have that could be used to guaranty your loan. Sometimes you can get them to use the assets of the business, such as the washers and dryers, but they may request your home or any other assets you have.

FUTURE FINANCIAL DATA

All businesses are required to supply financial projections data. Most of the time, lenders will want to see what you expect your company to be able to do within the next five years. Each year's documents should include forecasted income statements, balance sheets, and cash flow statements. For the first year, you should supply monthly or quarterly projections. After that, you can stretch it to quarterly and/or yearly projections for years two through five.

Finally, include a short analysis of your financial information. You may want to add graphs of your future revenue.

9. APPENDIX

The appendix would include:

- Credit history (personal & business)
- Resumes

- Product pictures
- Letters of reference
- Details of market studies
- Relevant magazine articles or book references
- Licenses or permits
- Legal documents
- Copies of leases
- Building permits
- Contracts
- List of business consultants, including attorney and accountant

Any copies of your business plan should be controlled, so keep a distribution record. This will allow you to update and maintain your business plan on an as-needed basis.

• • •

Another way to finance a laundromat is to take funds from a 401(k) or some other type of retirement account. This seems to be a more popular approach among the Baby Boomer generation and some of the early Generation X'ers, as you have to have a good-sized retirement account to fund a new business.

One way to do it is to simply cash out your 401(k) or whatever type of retirement account you have. The problem is you will have to pay income tax and early withdrawal penalties, so it's best to consult with an accountant to see how much you will need to set aside for taxes and penalties. Try not to think of it as spending your retirement, but as moving money from one investment to another. This new investment may or may not carry a higher risk. You need to determine your comfort level.

Another option is to create a corporation and use your retirement funds to buy stock in your company, which you can do without penalties. There are companies that specialize in this very thing. It's a little more complicated and there are certain procedures to follow, but it's another option. I won't go into much detail as I am not too familiar with the process, but as always, due diligence needs to be done with this option. Speak to your accountant and make sure it will work with your situation.

How about a home equity loan? They seem to be a little tough to get these days, but if your credit is in good shape and you have equity in your home, you should be able to get a loan. This was more popular before the recession and the banking collapse. All you had to do was buy a house and wait six months and you had $50,000 in equity. That equity all but disappeared in the months to come, but at the time it worked out well for some people. Of course, this debt service needs to be figured into your pro-forma.

There are a couple of different types of equity loans.

First is the HELOC, or home equity line of credit. With this loan the interest rate is adjustable, usually based off of prime, but is historically low. Plus, you only pay interest on the balance that you use. They will issue a credit limit, such as $100,000, but if you only need $75,000 you still have $25,000 you can use if needed at a later date.

To do this, simply write a check. Payments are interest-only for a set period of time, but you can pay more if you choose. It's best to commit early to paying off your debt within five years and make payments to do so. The nice thing is that if the unexpected happens, you can tap into the line of credit without going to the bank. I personally like this loan product the best because during slow months like December you can pay a little less and make up for it when business comes back in February.

The other type of home equity loan is called a second mortgage. With this, you're taking out a loan for a predetermined amount and paying it back over a set period of time. The interest rate tends to be a little higher, but it's still less than a business loan.

Let's say you have enough equity to get a loan for $100,000. At closing you will get a check for $100,000, for which you will have a term anywhere from five to 30 years at usually a fixed rate. Your payments will be the same every month unless you make additional principal payments. You could either put some of that cash in the bank for a rainy day fund or use it all to fund your business.

Some of these loans have a balloon payment at the end. You may have a 15-year loan with a 30-year amortization, meaning that your payments are calculated as if you have a 30-year loan. At the end of the 15 years, you either have to pay the balance in full, the balloon, or refinance.

I used to think that I could just refinance at a later date, but then the bottom fell out for the lenders and their belts got tighter. You don't need a foreclosure because they suddenly think you're a bad credit risk. It's wise to do your due diligence and get outside consultation on the different home loan products out there.

My favorite types of financing are both seller financing and private money. Private money can be tough if you don't know anybody with a little extra cash. However, I have heard of people putting ads in the paper asking for money with good payback terms. Generally, you are going to pay a higher rate for this type of loan.

In my opinion, seller financing needs to be part of the deal. I want the seller to have a little skin in the game to keep him honest. They know you are going to have a hard time getting money anyway, so don't be afraid to ask. I would ask for them to carry the whole loan over seven years at a good rate and see what they say. The worst they can do is say no. If that happens, ask for a little less. If they still say no, then I would ask them directly how much they would carry to meet their comfort level.

Then, say something like, "If this business is everything you say it is, then you shouldn't have a problem with a small loan. I shouldn't have any problems paying it back, right?" They should carry something.

Some owners may want to have a life insurance policy on you. They do have an insurable interest, so a policy can be issued. But do you feel comfortable with that situation? If the seller is tied to the mafia in any way, I would avoid the life insurance policy, as they may have you wacked. In some cases they may want to have a lien on an asset that you have, like a rental property or your personal home.

In many cases you'll get funding from multiple sources. You may have the seller carry $25,000, have a HELOC for 50,000, and borrow $25,000 from your 401k. Whatever you need to do to fund your dream, make it happen.

CHAPTER 10
YOU OWN IT. SO NOW WHAT?

When I first took ownership I had no idea of what to do with myself.

The employees of the place I took over seemed to be in limbo and there were rumors that I was going to fire everyone, which was the last thing I wanted to do. After all, they knew more about this place than I did. I needed them to teach me about the business.

I had gone through some training with the previous owner, but it didn't fully prepare me for everything I was about to encounter. Turns out, the last owner would let the employees pretty much run the laundromat on their own and I ended up losing two employees within the first few days. A few weeks later, three more left. They weren't happy with me wanting to have a say in my own business.

One of them actually changed the "last wash" time on the door because she didn't like working late and another would tan during his shift. They just did whatever they wanted to do.

In terms of improvements, take a good hard look at the laundromat before you decide on what to do first. Plan your work and make a list of priorities. When you first started researching the laundromat, you should have started developing a game plan. This will come in handy at this point, so put the plan to work. Every laundromat is different and will have different priorities.

In the first couple years, I did a lot to improve my laundromat. I noticed that the place looked dirty and dated, and it needed to be freshened up. I started with a real good cleaning.

Every little thing needed to be cleaned. All the ceiling fans had dust hanging from them and the carpeting had lots of stains. The men's restroom had little brown spots all over the ceiling and the exhaust fan was hanging down. There were hand-written signs all over the place on the walls, the washers and dryers, the changers, and the vending machines. On the tanning beds, the owner had simply taken black permanent marker and written directly on the beds themselves.

We went through the store and started to replace all the handwritten signs with ones we either purchased or made on the computer. We scrubbed off the black marker and replaced it with labels from a label maker I purchased. There were also about a dozen plants in the store that needed to be repotted and trimmed.

The walls were white and plain, so we did some repainting. Everybody in the laundry industry hears that customers want a bright, clean laundromat. That's true, but it seems that owners always paint the walls white and put in horrible bright lighting. We toned it down a bit and put in some warmer earth-tone colors. Then, we painted the words "Tanning," "Alterations," "Coin Changers," and "Vending" over their respective areas on the walls. This helped people find their way around the store.

The Formica on the clothes folding tables was coming off, so we found a match at a local hardware store and started replacing the sides. The dry clean rack was falling off the wall, so we replaced it with a sturdy chrome rack. We also got some chrome wire shelving units for finished drop laundry orders. It seemed to add a nice look behind the counter and started to modernize things.

We put some shelving up to showcase the laundry detergents, dryer sheets, fabric softener, bleach, laundry bags, and stain removal products we were selling. I found that the local dollar store had the detergent and dryer sheets at the great price of only a dollar. You can even order by the case by going to DollarTree.com and looking for the Dollar Tree Direct link. These products alone doubled our over-the-counter sales.

Our 50 lb. and triple load washers are bolted to a concrete base. The bases had some horrible rubber cover that was falling off and trapping a bunch of dirt. We ended up stripping the base and painting it with garage floor paint. This gave us a nice clean look in front of the washers and was certainly worth the time and effort.

We also needed a menu for the wall, so we taped off a section and painted the wall with black chalkboard paint. We purchased some brightly colored chalk and had my wife, with her best penmanship, write our tanning, drop laundry, and dry cleaning prices on it. This cost us about $10 and it looked great. I didn't know if the previous owner had wanted his customers to guess the prices, but there was nothing in terms of signage.

• • •

When I first took over my laundromat, one of the first things I did was change some store policies. The previous owner refused to give refunds to customers. After the police showed up over an issue with a quarter, we changed that and we now give away free washes or dries for just about any problem, no questions asked. It makes for happy customers and avoids conflict.

We started to advertise on a quarterly basis. We did postcards and flyers, and even tried a cost-effective money mailer program in the neighborhood. It ended up driving a lot of sales to our tanning beds. With the new look and policies, word of mouth spread quickly.

Our revenues were going up and things were looking great for a couple of years, until I got some bad news. Someone was building a new laundromat just down the road.

The next chapter is all about what you should do when new competition comes along. You need to really dig deep to make improvements that your customers will be sure to notice.

CHAPTER 11
NEW COMPETITION

Before you start this process, you need to take a good look at yourself. Do you have what it takes to see it through?

To be honest, I have good days and bad days, but I need those bad days to spur my creativity. It's a process. I'll have a bad day with all these negative thoughts and the next morning a great idea will pop into my head. It keeps me from getting complacent.

Dealing with new competition is a lot of work. It may take several months to years for you to recover. You might be thinking that you want to sell now and be done with the whole thing before the inevitable happens. Just close the door, sell the equipment, and cut your losses.

Somehow I don't think this describes you, or you wouldn't be reading this book. However, you must look at each challenge from every angle, run each scenario out in your mind, and find the best route for you. You can do this, but it's going to be tough at times.

So the new competition was on its way. I found out from a note that an employee left me the day before. He had heard it from a customer and I immediately became a little angry. "Why didn't he call me yesterday so I could have started figuring things out?" I thought. Now I had to sit there for an entire 10-hour shift and couldn't do anything!

Those 10 hours felt like 10 days. I was thinking that the new place was going to drown me and my entire financial future passed before my eyes. My heart was pounding and I felt horrible. A million questions went through my head, like who was building, if they would have attendants, and whether or not there was room in our market for two laundromats.

Finally, I got a chance to drive by the new location and saw a storefront packed with washers and dryers on pallets. "At least they aren't open yet," I thought to myself.

I immediately started gathering information. What kind of washers were there? How many were there? How many dryers? Did I just count 35 stack dryers? I'm so dead!

I noticed that their parking situation was horrible, but the restaurant next to it was packed. They would have a lot of foot traffic at that location.

The next day I felt even worse. I needed to know who was building the place, so I started by calling the distributor who I thought sold the brand of washers I saw in the storefront. He told me that he didn't sell that brand in my state and that he didn't know anything about the new laundromat. He did recommend speaking to another distributor, but that person also didn't know anything. I was beginning to wonder what was going on.

I called my own distributor and asked him if he knew anything. He said that it was likely an out-of-state owner who bought the equipment from a non-local distributor.

I drove past again and saw a for-lease sign in the window, so I decided to call the leasing broker from my car. He told me that there was indeed going to be a laundromat there in about four months, but he would only say that it was an out-of-state investor building it and nothing more. I thanked him, hung up, and started banging my head on the steering wheel.

"Great," I thought. "I have four months until the end of my existence."

However, I didn't give up. If new competition happens to you, take the following steps to help maintain your survival.

1. GATHER AS MUCH INFORMATION AS POSSIBLE.

I was already a member of the Coin Laundry Association (CLA), so I looked for what information they had to help me out. If you're not a member of the CLA, you need to be, especially in this situation. I found an audio CD called "Fight or Flight," which I highly recommend.

After a few days, I realized that I couldn't just sit on the wayside and get run out of town. I needed to do something, so I decided to peruse two websites for laundry owners that had online forums. You can find them at PlanetLaundry.com (bulletin board) and CoinWash.com (forum). I figured that other owners had to have had similar troubles, so I sought their advice.

In one of the forums, I posted this:

I am new to this forum and have been a laundry owner for about 2 years. I am seeking advice because I have a new laundry being built about 1/2 mile down the road from my store. The last two years have been great. I have made many cosmetic improvements and have experimented with different types of advertising. I have increased revenues by 25% since I took ownership. I knew I would face a challenge such as this at some point, I just was hoping for at least 5 years under my belt before it happened.

From what I know, this is an out-of-state, multiple- store owner. I am going to assume they're paying cash and are a successful owner/operator.

Is there anyone out there who has had this happen to them or anyone who is opening a new store that can share some info as to what to expect for a grand opening? I would like to know what they may do as far as advertising and promotions. I would also like to know if anyone has lost business in this situation and what they did to get it back. I am an attended store and I am assuming they will be also.

Any help is appreciated.

Thanks!

Soon after, I received this response to my post:

Sounds like you are doing everything right when it comes to running your store. I would expect to lose 30-40% of your business. Good Luck!

That didn't sound too good, so I asked:

Is that 30% to 40% from personal experience or just what you heard someone else lost?

A different person posted this:

I believe he knows first-hand, as do I.

I responded:

Were you able to get any of that business back? And if so, what did you do to get it back? Or did you just learn to live with less business?

Another user posted that 30-40 percent sounded right, and another stated that he was in the same situation, but because he owned the building he was in good shape. Then, another person started an argument over owning a building and others jumped into that discussion. It got off-track quickly.

"Does anybody have some good solid advice?" I thought. "HELLO, I'M DYING OVER HERE. CAN ANYBODY HELP ME?!"

I learned that I was going to lose some business, but still didn't know what I should do to keep revenue up. Forums are a great source of information, I have learned a lot from them, but they can't provide everything. Most owners are just as lost as you are in this situation.

2. Seek out other local owners who may have had a similar problem.

I had better luck with some owners of local laundromats than I did with the forums because I could ask questions face-to-face.

I had met some local owners at a distributor event, including one person who had a couple of laundries in a smaller college town. This owner had someone build a new laundromat a few miles up the road from one of his locations a couple of years earlier. Keep in mind that in smaller rural communities, a few miles is the equivalent to several blocks in an urban setting.

This owner told me that when the competition first moved in, he saw no changes in his revenue, but about 10 months later he noticed that he was down about 25 to 30 percent. The numbers had slowly decreased, so he hadn't caught on right away.

He told me that he was able to get his business back by doing time-of-day pricing and put signage inside and outside of the store. On Tuesday, Wednesday, and Thursday, he had a reduced price on his 18 lb. washers. Since he was a 24-hour store and his competition was a mega-laundry open 7 a.m. to 10 p.m., he was able to keep those prices for an entire 72-hour period.

He said it took some time to get the business back, but eventually he recovered. He said that his revenues were now higher than what they were before the other place opened. It was nice to hear that somebody actually did something and succeeded.

Another way I have met local laundry owners has been with the letters of interest I send out. One of the people I met this way was the owner of a huge laundromat that did a ton of business, perhaps close to $400,000 per year or more. The place was on a very busy street, had great parking, and lots of equipment. However, it was in a rough neighborhood and the customers were pretty hard on the store. It needed work, but that didn't seem to bother him or his customers.

A while back, someone had built a new laundromat about a mile and a half away from him and he said it affected his sales by about 30 to 40 percent. He hadn't done any advertising or promotions to get his customers back, as he felt that his street was busy enough that he didn't need to invest in it. He told me that he might do 25-cent washes one day a week just to upset the other owner.

This place needed a lot of work, as people were smoking and there were "out of order" signs everywhere. The walls were dirty, floor tiles were broken, and the store was a mess. If he had put some effort into improving his place, I think he would have been much more successful in keeping his customers. He just didn't do anything. Often times, seeing what someone didn't do, but should have, is just as educational.

You need to talk to people, including those outside of the industry. It helps the process and they might have some great advice.

3. Get all the information you can about the person building the laundromat.

Go about this in a nice way by calling the distributors in your area and asking if they are working with the new place. If so, ask about the owner, whether or not it's his or her first laundromat, and when the place is going to open.

Don't stir the pot or make any claims or accusations. The best thing you can do is find a way to compete. The distributor is either going to have some information for you or not, so take what you can get.

Do not underestimate the owner of the new laundromat. Maybe he or she is very experienced and has a ton of cash to throw around. Plan for the worst and don't just sit there and wait for them to go out of business. The new person might actually know how to run a business.

In my situation, I didn't even know what state the new owner was coming from, so I had to be very resourceful. When the guy pulled the permit, I called the city and asked who it was. The city gave me the company's name and stated that the company also owned the building. Once I had a name, I looked it up on the Internet and got an address and phone number.

This was progress. I now knew what state the new owner was coming from, so I visited that state's Department of Financial Institutions website. There, I searched for the company and found the name of the actual owner. I did a Google search and was able to find some old newspaper articles that explained how he had purchased the strip mall down the road from me, and why.

I also found his MySpace page, which didn't help much, but was interesting. He was a little old to be on MySpace, but to each his own. I prefer Facebook.

Anyway, I was able to find some good information and what type of personality the guy had. He was not going to run his new business, as that was beneath him. He would have employees and managers doing the work for him. He was too rich to fail and close up shop, but it was possible that he wouldn't get a good return on his investment and he would sell it off.

Another person I knew in the business suggested I call him up or go over and meet him. He even said I should talk about my business and tell him where I stand on pricing. I personally don't agree with this advice and I wouldn't recommend trying it. Don't give the competition any ammunition. Besides, you can be sure that this person has been in your laundromat and he or she already knows how you run your business and where you stand on pricing.

4. EVALUATE YOUR LAUNDROMAT

You need to evaluate your laundry. Really take a step back and look at it objectively. This involves asking yourself some questions.

Have a friend come in and give you their honest opinion. Do you have enough equipment? Is your equipment all working and presentable? Can you still read the instructions on the front of the washers and dryers? Do your walls need to be painted? Is your floor in good condition? Does it need to be stripped and resealed or replaced? Is your lighting adequate? How do your bathrooms look? They better be spotless, as that's one of my gauges on how well a business is being run.

Is your laundromat really clean? Look in every corner, between your washers, and at the ceiling. The new store will be spotless, is yours? Are your store hours clearly marked? Do you have good signage? Are your signs professional? Are your prices clearly marked? I can't tell you how many laundries I go in and they don't even have a sign telling you how many minutes you get on the dryers.

Do you feel safe in your laundromat? Are there signs of vandalism? If I go into a laundry and there is obvious vandalism or signs asking to not vandalize, I automatically do not feel safe. If this is the case, you need to have better security. Sometimes just having better lighting is the key, but I do think that every business today needs to have security cameras.

Video surveillance systems are more affordable now than ever. There should be plenty of cameras out in the open so that people know they're there. There also needs to be a notice on the front door stating that your business has video surveil-lance and is monitored 24 hours a day. Most systems can be networked so you can view your laundromat from an Internet connection.

When shopping for video systems, go bigger than what you think you need. Often, after installing cameras, you'll find that you'll want a couple more. Also, get a hard drive that's bigger than what you think you need, which gives you more storage and allows you to view recordings from a couple of weeks past.

If your laundromat is unattended, you might need to have

someone check in more often or have someone there during busy times. Perhaps kids are coming in everyday after school and keeping your customers away. If you have video surveillance you will be able to spot trouble much more quickly.

Other things you need to evaluate are comfort and seating situations. Do you have enough folding tables? Do your customers have someplace to sit? Is there reading material, a TV, or at least music playing? Is the heat or A/C on? Do you have hot water?

How does your laundromat look to a person first setting foot inside it? A first impression is everything. Would you do your laundry there if you didn't own the place?

5. FIND OUT WHAT YOUR CUSTOMERS THINK OF YOUR LAUNDROMAT.

In my situation, the competition didn't come in four months, like they said it would. All the other owner did in that time was pull a permit, so the work hadn't even begun.

I, on the other hand, worked feverishly for those four months. I needed to know what my customers thought of my laundromat in order to figure out what I needed to improve.

My next step was to survey my customers. I bought a brand-new bicycle and placed it front and center on top of one of the bulk heads, between my big washers closest to the front door. To enter into a drawing to win the bike, customers needed to fill out a survey.

If you have an unattended laundry take a picture of the prize and have posters made. Place the poster in the front window and hang a couple more in the laundry. Leave the surveys out with a pen and a box to put them in.

I had surveys made in both English and Spanish, on a half-sheet of bright orange card stock, front and back.

Here is a sample:

Name_____ Phone #_____
Address_____City_____State_____Zip_____

1. Do we have enough washers available when you need them?
☐all the time   ☐most of the time   ☐sometimes   ☐I always have to wait

2. Which washers do you use the most?
☐super wash 50lb   ☐triple load   ☐white neptune front load   ☐top load

3. Which washers do we need more of?
☐super wash 50lb   ☐triple load   ☐white neptune front load
☐top load   ☐you have enough

4. Should we add larger washers than what we currently have?   ☐yes   ☐no

5. Do we have enough dryers available when you need them?
☐all the time   ☐most of the time   ☐sometimes   ☐I always have to wait

6. Which dryer do you use the most?   ☐50lb large   ☐30lb triple

7. Should we add more dryers?   ☐yes   ☐no   ☐you have enough

8. Which should we add more of?

☐50lb large   ☐30lb triple   ☐both   ☐you have enough

9. Is our store clean?   ☐yes   ☐no

10. Are our attendants helpful?   ☐yes   ☐no   ☐I don't need their help

11. How did you find us?   ☐from friend or family   ☐yellow pages
☐post card   ☐mailer/coupon   ☐just knew you were here   ☐flyer

12. Comments / What can we do to serve you better?
_____
_____
_____
_____

Signature_____ Date_____

I would tally the results on each Friday and then again on Monday. That way, I could see if my weekend customers felt the same as my customers during the week.

We had a good response, with over 300 people filling out the survey. These were the results:

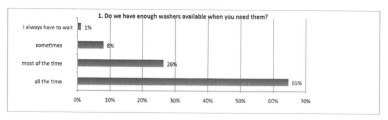

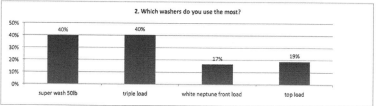

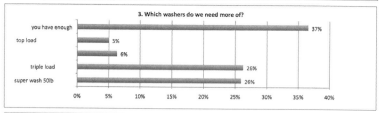

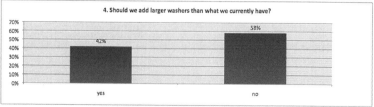

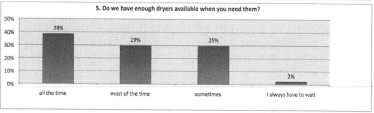

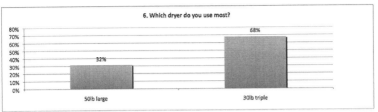

6. Which dryer do you use most?

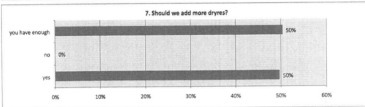

7. Should we add more dryres?

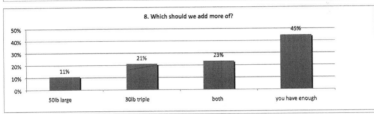

8. Which should we add more of?

9. Is our store clean?

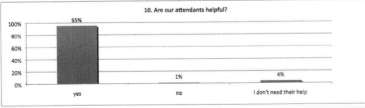

10. Are our attendants helpful?

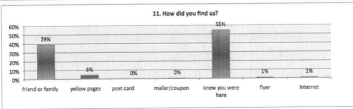

11. How did you find us?

Now that I had all this data, I had to figure out what it all meant. Here is how I interpreted the survey answers:

- We seemed to have enough washers and customers really used the bigger ones. About half thought we needed more of the bigger variety of washers. It would be an expensive fix, but I had room.
- Most people were able to find a dryer when they needed one, but more than half thought we needed more dryers. This concerned me because my competition would have twice the drying capacity that I did.
- We were definitely clean and the attendants were helpful.
- Word of mouth seemed to be the best advertising that we had.

I did notice that on the weekends my customers tended to want more dryers, but my weekday customers thought I had enough of everything.

Some of the comments asked us to add more machines. Others asked for low prices or more TVs and things for kids to do while parents were doing laundry. Someone even suggested a cafeteria and an ATM machine. Even though we got high marks with cleanliness, some comments stated that we should replace some broken floor tiles.

Many comments, on the other hand, said that we should keep doing what we were doing. Overall I think this was a good learning experience and I got some great ideas. Evaluations not only gave me good feedback, but also sent a message to my customers that I cared about their opinions.

1. GIVE YOUR CUSTOMERS SOME OF WHAT THEY ASKED FOR.

Your customers have given you some great tips, so take action and use them.

I began to consider some of the suggestions and thought about adding a couple 50 lb. stack dryers and some 80 lb. washers. I called my distributor and asked for pricing, but found that it would be too expensive. If I was going to lose customers, which was inevitable, I could go broke trying to pay off the loan it would require. I decided against the new equipment for the time being.

If money wasn't an issue, I would have added the equipment. Unfortunately it was an issue.

I really needed to do something about the floor, so I got some quotes and ended up replacing all my carpeting with tile. It made a big difference. I also pulled the carpeting off of the lower portions of the wall and installed drywall. After the improvements, the place was starting to look great!

A few of the comments stated that the kids needed more to do. We added books, more toys, additional children's seating, and installed a high-definition TV on the wall to play kids' movies all day. I also replaced the other TV with a large-screen high-def one.

I spent over $10,000 on these upgrades, but it was worth it. The laundromat had a brand-new feel and the customers loved it.

2. IMPROVE YOUR BOTTOM LINE.

I figured that the new laundromat was going to have more efficient equipment than me, so I needed to look into lowering some of my utility expenses.

We had already ruled out equipment upgrades, so I started examining some other ways to save energy. I put a timer on my water heater and my outdoor lighted sign. I upgraded the interior lighting to more efficient bulbs and ballasts. I saved quite a bit right there and my electric bill went down immediately. While I was at it, I had the lighting specialist put in a more natural light bulb, which made the place seem more comfortable and less like a drug store.

Then, I cleaned out the dryer ducts, as less friction makes the machines run more efficiently. All of these changes dropped my bottom line and I was happy to be saving money. Looking to save more, I went down my list of expenses and began calling every one of my billers to see if they could cut my rates.

You should definitely give this a try. Explain your situation to them and tell them you may have to cancel their service if they don't lower your rates. Call your insurance provider and look at your plan. Can you raise the deductible? Call around and get other quotes and see if your current providers can match them. If not, switch over.

It's your money, so get creative. Sometimes all you need to do is ask and you'll get results.

3. TRAIN YOUR EMPLOYEES.

Employee training is a never-ending process. I am one of those business owners who is always changing or adding something, which seems to keep everyone on their toes.

I had always done weekly bulletins for my employees, but in the situation in which I found myself, it was more important than ever. We needed to have the best customer service possible and we couldn't afford to have anyone leaving the laundromat upset.

If anyone had an issue with anything, whether it was our fault or theirs, we needed to make it right. We don't have to be the judge and the jury, but we need to help the customer. Problems are nothing more than opportunities and have an opportunity to turn negative situation into a positive one. If a customer leaves the laundromat upset, I can guarantee they will be talking trash to everyone they know.

If we turn it into a positive and go the extra distance to solve the problem, that customer will leave and tell ten of their friends how we went above and beyond to help them. After all, most of our customers found us through word of mouth, so let's give them something good to talk about.

If a customer comes up and says that she thinks there is something wrong with our dryers because her clothes aren't drying, we need to look at the dryer. If it is working properly we need to educate the customer on how long an average load takes to dry. Most importantly, we need to give them a little extra time on the dryer.

If a customer over-soaps a washer, we need to tell him or her how much soap to use and rewash the clothes at no charge. I truly believe it's some of the best advertising you can have.

Once the new competition opens up, you'll need to sit down and talk to your employees about what to say and not say. I didn't tell my workers about the new place until it opened. Yes, I was a little paranoid, but the last thing I needed was my employees advertising for the new laundromat by talking about it with customers. I told my employees that the new place might affect business for a while, but that we must be the best at the things we could control.

I created an employee training manual detailing all of our store's procedures. There is a section on duties for each shift, including what should be done and when. I have a bathroom and a washer cleaning policy, and all of the daily tasks that need to be completed.

We also have a process for drop laundry that includes how to check in an order from the write-up slip, how to weigh the order, and what to do for pick-up. There's a video I got from the CLA that demonstrates proper wash and fold procedures. I also included the processes for dry cleaning, the cash register, tanning booths, customer complaints, and even a trouble-shooting guide with pictures on how to deal with common equipment mishaps.

One of the most important pieces of employee relations is to have a name and phone list located in an easy-to-find location. I keep my vendors list in the same place, so if I'm going to be out for a few days, my employees can find the right people to contact if something goes wrong.

We must also address the fact that being a laundry attendant can be a little boring at times, as it's not really a job that pays great and has many advancement opportunities. With that in mind, I try to throw in a few perks. I allow my employees to do their laundry for free, even during their shift if everything else is done. I also let them tan for free and buy lotions at a reduced cost.

Remember, a happy employee is an effective employee.

4. RAMP IT UP!

When you find out about incoming competition, you'll likely have some time before they open their doors. They're also going to have to start from scratch with no customers. You already have the customers. All you need to do is keep them.

Well, whether you like it or not, you will lose some, but how many depends on you. I have found that if I really increase the amount of customers I have coming into my store before the other place opens, it won't be so bad to lose some when the time comes.

For example, try to increase your customer base by 25 percent before they open. Then, when it comes time, if you lose 25 percent, you'll break even. It won't be easy, but it's a good way to approach it. Did I ramp up 25 percent? No, but I gave it a try and I did gain quite a few new customers.

5. DO SOME MARKETING.

Speaking of gaining customers, in order to get people into your laundromat, you need to create buzz. How do you do that? By using some of the marketing techniques detailed below:

Word of Mouth

As I found out from my survey results, "friends and family" and "we just knew you were here" were the most popular reasons for people coming into my laundry.

If you're doing a good job, people will talk. And if you're doing a bad job, people will talk even more. The bottom line is that people will talk about your business whether you like it or not, so give them something good to talk about.

The best way to produce good word of mouth is to have a

clean, comfortable, and safe laundry that has all of its equipment working. It sounds simple, but 75 percent of the laundries I walk into have "out of order" signs on at least three or four pieces of equipment. Most places are dark, scary and need lighting or paint. I can't imagine anyone wanting to go in there.

Having good word of mouth may require some employee training, and perhaps some owner training. You should have a written policy on how to handle customer problems, including making sure you never prejudge anyone. Don't assume that someone is trying to take advantage of you.

One day I came in to my laundry and the employee on duty told me about a customer who said he put quarters in three washers and they never started. The employee told him that she was only paying for one of the washers.

The customer got very upset and started arguing with her, saying that we ripped him off. She then told him that she felt like she was the one getting ripped off. She told me she didn't think he put money in any of the washers.

So who is right?

When I came in, this guy was huffing and puffing as he was walking throughout the store. He was bad-mouthing the employee to everyone he saw in the store. Obviously, this was poor word of mouth.

So really, who cares who was right? Let's not be judge and jury. Maybe the customer was taking advantage of us, but that was okay. We didn't know for sure, so we needed to give him some free washes and take a small loss.

I'd rather give away three washes because of the slight chance that this person was taking advantage of us. After all, some customers put in all of the quarters but one in the washers they are going to use. Then they add soap and whatever else before putting in the last coin. Sometimes these people are so slow that the washer actually times out and acts as if nothing was ever put in them. I don't know what happened, but I don't want to lose any customers, period.

The point is that we needed to give the customer something good to talk about. Most people are honest; the percentage of people who will take advantage of you is small.

If you have an unattended laundry and someone calls or fills out a problem card with an issue, consider sending them a vending-size box of detergent with their refund. They may brag about it to their friends. Also, make the refund timely, within a day of the initial complaint.

I've also found that people love giveaways and it really gets them talking about my laundromat in a positive way. I give away a bicycle every few months and get hundreds of entries each time I do it.

The bottom line is that if you do what you're supposed to be doing and throw in a few extras, people will talk and revenue will go up. It's the best advertising money can't buy.

The Banner

After I heard about the other laundromat, I immediately put out a large banner visible for cars driving past. We also have a nearby apartment complex and I wanted to make sure to grab the attention of any new movers.

I highly recommend having a banner, even if it simply says "COIN LAUNDRY" and shows your hours. The main idea is to get people to look your way when they normally would not. Use bright colors like red and yellow to make sure this happens.

Keep the banner up for a couple months before taking it down. After a few weeks, put the banner up in a different spot to keep things fresh.

Another tip is to have slits cut into the banner. The first time around I learned the hard way that without these slits, the banner acts like a big wind sail.

If you're renting the location, make sure your landlord is okay with the banner. Mine wasn't a fan of it until I explained to him that if I didn't draw business, I wouldn't be paying my lease. He seemed to understand after that.

The Internet

The Internet is an important tool for any business owner looking to attract customers. In fact, right now businesses can't afford not to have an online presence.

I was able to create a simple website using a template provided by Yahoo! that was very easy to use. Microsoft Office Live has a similar program. This will only cost you a few dollars per month.

Crafting the site took a lot of time, but was worth the effort. I submitted it to every search engine I could find. Now, every time someone searches for laundry in my area, my business is the first to pop up in the results. The more content and links you add, the more searchable your site will be.

This tactic, called search engine optimization, is what takes the most time. You have to strategically plan the words on your home page and have the correct metatags encoded in your site.

I also went to dozens of online directories and created free listings with descriptions of our services. I also included photos of the laundromat and had some of my best customers go online and give us a positive review.

After my site was up, I created a Facebook page for my business and linked it to the website. I put up signs in my laundry promoting my page, encouraging customers to become my Facebook fans by offering some freebies like detergent and other offers. Again, make use of this free advertising.

If you think that your customers are too low-income to be connected to the Internet, think again. Everyone has a mobile phone these days, even if they cannot afford the web access. If you have free WiFi, your customers can use their phones to connect to the Internet, which only gives them another reason to use your laundromat.

You definitely need to be on the web if you have a hotel near your location. Travelers use the Internet to find everything when they're going on vacation, and many will need a laundromat. Make sure they can find you online.

Post Cards

In terms of paid advertising, post cards have resulted in the most success for me. Mailing to apartment complexes within a one-mile radius of my store works the best. I have experimented with venturing further out, but keeping it close has yielded better returns.

You may have to experiment a little also to find what works best for you, as every neighborhood is different. You need to know what types of dwellings are in your neighborhood, which can be done by running a demographic report. Do you have houses, duplexes, town houses, multifamily buildings, or condos? Do you have a lot of low-income residents in your neighborhood? *The CLA's 2006 laundry customer profile* states that 53 percent of all renters who use self-service laundries have incomes below $30,000. These are your customers, so you'll want to target them.

When you send out post cards, I recommend a saturation mailing in which you mail a card to everyone living on a particular postal carrier route. The post card company will be able to give you the route and how many apartment dwellings and homes are in it. I have found that a saturation mailing is the least expensive.

You can target almost any type of audience, such as low-income, renter, homeowner, or families with children. You name it, they can target it. The post card company will have mailing lists for almost any combination. The more selective you are, the more you may pay for the mailing list.

Once you know who you are mailing to, create a promotional piece that will grab people's attention. Your post card company can assist with this, but big and bright work best. You could design a post card of your own on a brightly colored 6 x 11-inch card, which will definitely stand out in the mail. I personally wouldn't use a card smaller than a 5.5 x 8.5-inch card, which is a more standard size.

Once you get the right size, figure out what to say. Keep it short, use bold print, have an offer, and highlight some of your qualities. According to *the CLA's 2006 laundry customer profile,* the following factors influence customers' decisions about choosing a laundromat:

Enough Machines Available	85%
Cleanliness	81%
Feeling Safe and Secure	75%

Store Hours	74%
Big Machines	72%
Distance from Home	68%
Vend Price	65%
Attendant on Duty	62%
Parking Available	61%

Build your post card around the most important customer wants. Highlight a few key things that your laundromat does better than the competition while integrating some of the top customer influences. You could mention how many washers you have and say that you are "Safe, Secure & Clean," incorporating the top three customer influences.

Remember to keep these post cards short and concise. I would include a small map so people know how to get there, complete with an address and phone number in bold. Add your store hours and website, if you have one.

In order to know how successful your post card campaign is, find a way to track it. Giveaways are a great way to do this, so make an offer like, "BRING IN THIS CARD FOR FREE DETERGENT THIS SATURDAY THE 00/00/00!" Then provide everyone who brings in the card that day with some free vending-size detergent.

If you are unattended then I would do a promotion for one or two days, then you need to be in the Laundromat those days. If you are an attended Laundromat I would do the promotion for two or three weeks.

The better the giveaway, the better your rate of return will be. I have tried giving away a free wash with the purchase of a wash in a single loader and didn't get many takers. I have also tried a free wash in any top loader or double loader with no purchase, which resulted in a little better return, although it was still pretty small. These were both on small cards about a quarter size of a sheet of paper.

I then switched to a half sheet, which is a 5.5 X 8.5-inch card, and gave away a free wash in any washer all the way up to our 60 lb. machines. The return rate was much better.

To track the return, you need to do some math. Let's say we send out 1,500 post cards in a specific area and we received 79 cards from people who redeemed them. Take the amount of redeemed cards and divide it by the total mailing:

$$79 / 1,500 = .053 \text{ (or 5.3\%)}$$

Our return would be 5.3 percent, which is a successful campaign. Anything over 2 percent is good. Mailings generally have lower rates of return, so you must send out a lot of them and have some good offers. Be consistent and do multiple mailings and your rates of return will improve with time.

If you think this is a waste of money, consider this: Using some common industry assumptions according to the CLA, we can say that the average laundry customer spends about $450 to $550 per year or more. If we want to make $150,000 in annual gross sales, we would need 333 customers. If we already got 79 from our mass mailing, that's a great return on investment.

I also track the number of new customers by simply asking if they have ever been here before. You should train your employees to do the same. In a recent mailing I had 15 new customers, which doesn't sound like much, but in the long run I could be making $6,000 from the increased business. Fifteen new customers multiplied by the low average ($450) equals $6,750 in annual sales, which is not bad.

I like to track everything, so I also track which type of washer they used, which postal carrier route the customer came from, and how many were redeemed each week. You will be able to see which areas result in a better return rate or more new customers.

One thing I should note is that you need to pay extra special attention to the legal information on the post cards, such as the fact that it's "limit one per customer" (or family), and so on. People will find loopholes, don't let it bother you too much because the percentage of those taking advantage is small. Sometimes I get people who stole their neighbor's coupons and have everyone in the family come in one at a time, each with one load of laundry. Later I'll see them all sitting together at a table, but I don't let it get to me.

It may take a while to find your niche when it comes to post card advertising. Experiment and find which target areas and card designs work best for you.

Door Hangers

I have had some success with door hangers, but they're not as good as post cards. I usually use my post cards art work and have my printer put it on a door hanger. Just like the post cards, bigger is better.

There are a few different types of door hangers. One has a doorknob hole, one has a rubber band attached, and another just sticks to the door. The sticky ones won't blow away in the wind like the others. Plus, you can stick them on car windows.

I get a better rate of return with the sticky version because they stand out better. For great "stick-it" door hangers at a reasonable price, visit AdeasPrinting.com.

In my area, I have a lot of big apartment buildings I can't get into because they have locked entrances. Because of that, I'm limited to putting them on single-family homes, duplexes, and town homes. I try to hit areas that seem to have more of a rental population.

I can usually do about five hundred in an afternoon, but it's a lot of walking around. There are companies that will do this for you, but I do it myself to save money. I send post cards to multi-family buildings and distribute door hangers everywhere else.

Other forms of advertising

Another advertising tactic is to do a mass mailing that features some kind of promo pack that has other advertisers included. They're usually affordable and I have had mixed results with them.

You could also try the back of the receipt tape at a local large retailer, but I have found this to be expensive with little or no return. Newspaper, radio, and TV have all been too expensive for me to try, so I can't really comment on that. Just keep in mind that it's an option.

Generally, I have found that a laundromat's customers are coming from an area within one to four miles of the location, so you need to advertise in your target area. Perhaps a billboard will work for you, or a coupon on the menu of a popular local restaurant.

Church bulletins are affordable and people do read them. I spend a good amount on the yellow pages, but have found it hard to track because I can't tell how many customers have been driven to my store by it. Every time I think to cancel my yellow page ad, I chicken out. I just hate to lose business and with the new laundry coming, I didn't want to take any chances.

I have found that with advertising that every sales person seems to know your business better than you. I think if they where actually counting the money and cutting the checks, they may see things a little different.

When you are talking to someone about advertising, never commit right then and there. Take some time to think about it. I hate things with contracts and it makes me believe that they have an inferior product, so if the advertiser wants a contract with a specific time period, I would advise you to negotiate the time down. Tell them you will do three months at a time.

If the advertisement works, they shouldn't have any worries. I just don't want to commit to anything for a year and find out a few months later that it isn't working at all or that they stretched the truth in the sales pitch.

6. WHAT DO YOU DO ONCE THE COMPETITION OPENS?

Bomb the place!

Okay, that's a joke, so don't do that. Hopefully by now you have some peace of mind about this whole situation. Get the thoughts about going over there and washing bags of quick set concrete out of your mind.

The first thing you should know is that the other place is going to do some type of promotional pricing. This may last a month to several months. People have a natural curiosity and your customers will want to try out the new place, so accept that and move on.

At this stage in the game, try to spend more time in your

store, especially if it's an attended laundromat. This will give you a chance to listen to your customers. I trained my employees not to tell anybody about the other laundromat, but if they heard something to let me know.

If a customer commented that it was slow in my place, I told my employees to respond that it always slowed down this time of year or this time of day. I didn't want to mention the competition, as I could just imagine one of my employees saying, "We've been slow since that new laundromat opened." That would only make the customer curious about the other place.

Keep monitoring your sales. Have they changed much? When my competition first opened, my sales went down 33 percent in their second week, but snapped back to normal the following week. It has been up and down.

Many of my customers were telling me that they didn't like the new laundromat down the street. That was a good sign, and gave me some ideas on how to highlight my strengths in my next round of advertising.

The important thing is to keep your eyes on your profit and not so much your volume of clients. Don't make any reactionary changes in pricing, as the other place will be cheaper than you at first. Remember that they will eventually have to raise their prices to be profitable. Don't engage in a price war.

Try not to drive past the other store every day because it will drive you crazy. Just because they have customers doesn't mean they are all yours. They will expand the market and pull some people out that you may not have reached.

On the topic of expanding markets, it's time you do the same, including the use of some marketing techniques. The week my competitor opened, I mailed out 1,500 post cards.

Two weeks later, I sent another 1,500. This reminded people I was still there and diluted the competition's grand-opening mail campaign a bit.

After his grand opening mailing ended, I sent out another 3,000 post cards. This helped me keep my name out there.

I also walked the neighborhood and distributed door hangers. These 2,500 pieces added to my direct mailings, which meant I had made contact with 8,500 households in just a few months.

Don't lay down to the competition. Stay consistent and aggressive in your marketing.

12. When to implement Plan B.

After several months, I found myself down about 8 to 13 percent from where I had been a year earlier.

I had been advertising consistently, doing about 500 door hangers per week and sending out about 3,000 post cards every other month. I was doing my best to keep my losses at a minimum. I couldn't afford to keep advertising at that pace for much longer, so I had to stop the post cards after a few months.

I decided to concentrate on door hangers because they were more affordable, and right now I try to get out about 1,000 door hangers a month.

If you're in this situation, you may want to stay on this path or try a different one. A good way to mix things up is to go after the market of people using the laundry rooms in apartment complexes. There are a lot of these people, but we must overcome the fact that it's more convenient for them to do laundry on-site.

First we need to understand what they have in the laundry

rooms in the complexes. If you ask the residents, you'll find that the rooms are small and dirty. People will remove your laundry and throw it on top of the washer so they can use it. Machines are almost always in use or just sitting with clothes in them.

Some of these apartment laundry rooms are card-operated, but users must go to the rental office to recharge them and it's not always open. On top of that, people have actually been assaulted in these rooms and some are afraid to use them.

So how do we get some of that market? We tell them that we are safe, secure, and clean. We have large capacity washers and a ton of them, which means they can get all of their laundry done in two hours, not days. If that doesn't work, find out the complex's pricing and match it with time-of-day pricing.

Run that special two or three days a week and make sure people know about it by using banners, post cards, door hangers, and the proper signage. Give the promotion time to ramp up and you will get some of these people out of the laundry rooms and into your establishment.

If you have an attended laundry, one way to drum up business is to go after the drop laundry and commercial accounts. You can do this by hitting the street, going door to door, and promoting your business's commercial services. One owner I talked to said it's just a matter of how many doors you want to knock on. It is tough to do and you have to be persistent.

We will never know what the market will bear until we give it a shot. You can be sure that there is some business out there that you have overlooked.

CONCLUSION

We covered a lot of information in this book and I hope it was helpful.

In regards to my new competition, I hope they get what they are looking for. I truly do want them to succeed. Of course, I don't want it to be at my expense. I hope we both can succeed. I've come to realize that I need to concentrate on what I can control.

Above all, be sure to buy a laundromat that has potential to make good cash. Look over the numbers carefully and seek second opinions with people you know for some honest advice.

If possible, try to diversify your business. I have apart-ments to fall back on if I have to and I am always looking for other business opportunities. If one business is struggling, you can lean on the other for a while to make ends meet.

Perhaps you could keep your full-time job and run the laundry on the side. I know a few people who do that and it works well because they don't need the money from the laun-dromat to pay the bills. It's all extra cash and they have built a nice savings from the business.

You may want to go back and read some of the informa-tion we covered in this book, especially when you are looking at a location to buy. Revisit the pages on each topic to make sure you don't miss anything. I also suggest you read other books on this subject. Everyone has different twists on things and it's good to get as much information as you possibly can to make a sound decision.

Take a moment to visit my website at HowToBuyaLaundromat.com and look at some of the spreadsheets I have to offer, including more than what was provided in this book. They come with instructions and can be valuable tools. I'm always working on improving my spreadsheets, so check back every once in a while and see what's new.

Remember, all businesses carry a certain amount of risk, and some more than others. Calculate that risk and make sure it's one worth taking.

I wish you much success in your business search.

Made in the USA
San Bernardino, CA
13 October 2014